Gallery Books
Editor Peter Fallon

OLYMPIA AND THE INTERNET

Derek Mahon

OLYMPIA AND THE INTERNET

Gallery Books

Olympia and the Internet
is first published
simultaneously in paperback
and in a clothbound edition
on 28 September 2017.

The Gallery Press
Loughcrew
Oldcastle
County Meath
Ireland

www.gallerypress.com

ISBN 978 1 91133 710 2 *paperback*
      978 1 91133 711 0 *clothbound*

A CIP catalogue record for this book
is available from the British Library.

Olympia and the Internet receives financial assistance
from the Arts Councils of Ireland.

LOTTERY FUNDED

Contents

for Sarah

Going to the Pictures

'What's all the fuss about?' said Peter O'Toole when the critics panned his Old Vic *Macbeth* (1980). 'It's only a bloody play.' Orson Welles's film of the Scottish play was only a bloody film, but it scared the living daylights out of us youngsters when, ill-advisedly, we were taken to see it for educational reasons in 1951. I had to sleep with the light on for a week. Those witches! Macbeth himself (Welles), and the bit where his thugs chase the Macduff child with murderous intent: help! Thereafter it was mostly fruity-voiced British war films, some great of their kind it must be said — *The Cruel Sea* (1952), *The Dam Busters* (1954) — incomprehensible love stories which made sense only on later reflection, and westerns of course, each indistinguishable from the last. 'Going to the pictures', you saw a film once only in those pre-video days unless you went twice, or more indeed, as we did to *The Young Lions* (1958). Young lions ourselves, or so we liked to think (some of us were in the school cadet corps), this was our favourite; but with whom to identify? Clift, Dean Martin, Brando's troubled German? Belfast cinemas: our local Capitol, the Lyceum farther down the Antrim Road, the Troxy (the Troxy??) on the Shore Road; and then there were film *societies*. Are we 'fanatical about film'? No, even at that age we're discriminating about films. Some are fine; most, like most of anything, aren't up to much. (The distance from *Citizen Kane* to *Dumb and Dumber* is immense.) But I want to sideline the Hollywood product here — so much of it! — and remember instead the brainy stuff, film as 'art': *La Strada* (1954), Andrzej Wajda's *Ashes and Diamonds* (1958). Except for the likes of *Black Orpheus* (Brazil, 1959), it was mostly the European thing: Godard's *À Bout de Souffle* (1959) and so on. (Always annoys me, by the way, to see this translated as 'Breathless' when what it means here is 'Out of Breath', perhaps 'End of the Road' or even 'Running on Empty', titles since used by other directors.) High points, we're now in the sixties: Pontecorvo's *Battle of Algiers* (1965), Bergman's *Wild Strawberries* (1967), so outstanding in their very different ways they're both spared, for very different reasons, the captious house style of *Time Out Film Guide*.

I think my first realization that films are manufactured, and don't just drop from the sky, took place on a beach at St.-Malo, Brittany, in 1956 or so. We were on a school trip (Mont St.-Michel etc) and there, on the sand, was a British film crew making *True as a Turtle* (1957), dir. Wendy Toye. June Thorburn (b.1931), also in *The Cruel Sea* and many more, sat on a mat in a swimsuit waiting for camera action. We too waited, but nothing seemed to happen, so we left them to it; but I now knew films were *work*, and slow work into the bargain, an experience I was to know again at first hand when writing for TV in later years. Screen is an industry like any other; Hollywood, said Scott Fitzgerald, is 'a mining town in lotus land'. But artistic minds in Europe and elsewhere, while conscious of commercial imperatives, once espoused 'art-house' values, and that's the sort of thing we treasure and remember; the rest is 'entertainment', if sometimes of high quality. Art houses? The old Mayfair in Belfast; in Dublin the Astor and Corinthian, side by side on Eden Quay. The big pictures were screened in O'Connell St., the little ones at the Green on Stephen's Green or the Grafton in Grafton St., previously a 'News and Cartoon' cinema, Bugs Bunny etc. The history of these places is available in Jim Keenan's *Dublin Cinemas* (Picture House Publications, 2005), illustrated with many photos. He has an eye for architecture and décor, the visual experience of the cinemas themselves, the often ornate interiors of high-end houses like the Carlton and the Savoy, besides the vanished fleapits and local suburban venues. TV put paid to much of this; and now, in the internet age, the very idea of 'distribution' is a sort of anthropology. We download our old favourites, but it's not the same as the big screen; and even to say 'download' is to risk anachronism since anything high tech can be out of date in a month, a week, even overnight.

Old favourites? The best of the fifties and sixties were British, French and Italian: Tony Richardson's *The Entertainer* (1960), Olivier as Archie Rice ('Don't clap too hard, it's a very old building'), and *Tom Jones* (1963), both of them scripted, and brilliantly, by John Osborne, *The Entertainer* from his own play, *Tom Jones* from the Henry Fielding novel. Tom especially (Albert Finney) was a great favourite, epoch-making indeed in many respects, great fun at any rate: that raunchy supper scene with Joyce Redman, the talking to camera, the abrupt freeze frames, Micheál Mac Liammóir's rich, period-inflected VO narration: all very arch and 1960s. Very sixties too, in fact *the* British film of those years, John Schlesinger's *Darling* (1965), has had a curious reception history. *Time Out*, for example, takes a dim view: 'A leaden rehash of ideas from Godard, Antonioni and Bergman . . . Excruciatingly embarrassing at the time, it now looks grotesquely pretentious' and so on. No, no, no! It's a great film: strong story well told, terrific script by Frederic Raphael, first-rate cast: Julie Christie, Dirk Bogarde, Laurence Harvey. The title is odd, a sort of non-title; but the story of model Diana Scott's progress and 'success' in the advertising and media world of sixties London is always imaginative and never dull. The tragic arc of her career holds us from start to finish, the acting is superb; so why has it been dismissed? A reaction against the British 'New Wave' of the day? Diana, during a Paris trip, attends a strange party involving a scary truth game, *'une sorte de cinéma-vérité existentiel'* says the host, a phrase which could describe *Darling* itself, and of course certain *Cahiers du Cinéma* ideas, for these were the days of Truffaut *et cie*. The tedious, repetitious *Jules et Jim* (1961) could put you off Truffaut; but Louis Malle, now, there was a director: *Zazie dans le Métro* (1960) and the rest. These *auteurs* worked in America too in due course, Malle more interestingly than most: *Pretty Baby* (1977), *Atlantic City* (1980). There was always an American component in *Nouvelle Vague* thinking.

We saw the new millennium in from a Roman flat beside the Tarpeian Rock; all went up on the roof to watch the fireworks.

I'd been going to Rome in the autumn for a couple of years. Nice Caterina Salabè, scholar and translator, took me for a spin on her powerful, snarling Vespa. ('*Non fa rumore*', complained an Italian youth on trying an English model.) A fan of *La Dolce Vita* (1960), and indeed of the great Fellini generally, I'd thought of looking at various locations he'd used, imagining it would take me a few days to cover the ground. Not at all, said Caterina, we can do it this evening; and so we did. The historic centre, not large, is easily negotiable, so off we went (*vroom, vroom*) to the Trevi fountain and the rest, describing a circle and ending up in the Piazza Navona where, a cameo appearance in Fellini's *Roma* (1972), Gore Vidal remarks that it's 'as good a place as any to watch the end of the world'. It's a cinematic city. Anthony Burgess noticed 'the sense of an invisible camera recording everything, the border between the genuinely filmed and the potentially filmable not always easy to descry'. I tried to get this too in my own 'Roman Script' poem, script as in film script, where even the football-playing prisoners in the Regina Coeli (Trastevere) exercise yard are enrolled in the whimsical fun:

> *and we walk in reality, framed as virtuality,*
> *as in a film-set, Cinecittà, a cinema city*
> *where life is a waking dream in broad daylight*
> *and everything is scripted for our delight.*

La Dolce Vita, considered a bit naive by wised-up film historians, was a great thing in its day, what with that helicopter carrying the Christ figure over the roof tops, the sunbathing girls and bell-ringing city, in the unforgettable opening sequence. It retains, after fifty years, much of its original impact and much of its relevance; things have changed, but not significantly. 'Our ship is sinking,' said Fellini. 'It's happening in other countries too. There's the tragic fascination of watching a ship go down . . . We've finished one phase of history and haven't begun the next.'

La Dolce Vita was a substitute title: he'd wanted to call it *Babylon*, to emphasize the timeless element in 'a story wrongly thought to be only about contemporary phenomena'. The film has its dark depths for sure, and a long historical reach: the religious component, the organ, the castle, the fish, the angelic girl. If that monstrous fish in the last minutes (a giant ray?) could make organ music it would play, as Steiner (Alain Cuny) does at one point, the Bach Toccata and Fugue in D Minor with its deep rumble of origins. As for the angelic girl, this is of course Paola, the innocent fifteen-year-old whom Marcello likens to a painting in an Umbrian church, and whose smile fills the screen in the final frame. Rich in incident and surface effect, this long episodic film (166 mins), with its multinational cast and many distractions, pursues nonetheless a single unifying theme: the replacement of an older, organic life by technology of all kinds including film itself, from the chopper to the many cars and cameras: all those news photographers! The film contains within it an ironical critique of its own message and medium. The *paparazzi* in pursuit of the celebrities are themselves pursued by the film camera; the artful Paparazzo acquires something like celebrity status. Cameras chase cameras, all in black and white. Colour would have enhanced the 'entertainment' value perhaps, but would have seriously compromised the 'spiritual' dimension. Suggestions of historicity, documentary and a vague amateurism we associate with the monochrome option contribute to the Gothic mood and combine with the adventitious, unrehearsed, extemporaneous air of many scenes to create a forceful real-time, 'real life' atmosphere. A touch of 'amateurism', of the aleatoric, does no harm. It dispels, indeed, the monotony of technical perfection in this as in any art form.

Disruption of the conventional film 'grammar' works wonders, here as elsewhere. The sounds and imageries of the digital chocolate box wash over us; the eccentric things remain. I think of Eric Rohmer's *Die Marquise von O—* (1976), the Kleist story retold in a series of short scenes unspoilt by intrusive music, each crystal-clear composition instantly retrievable from visual memory — which brings me back to the business of literary adaptation. *Tom Jones*, in my own experience and that of my generation, was only one of many (even those Bogie movies were based on Chandler novels); there's a whole literature of the book-to-film enterprise. I was going to say page-to-screen, but all films start on the page, so there's nothing new about that. Monroe Stahr (Irving Thalberg), in *The Last Tycoon* (1976), tells the English novelist George Boxley (Aldous Huxley) about 'making pictures', as if the process were self-defining, without any serious writerly input, and Boxley himself an idiot. But, starting with a 'treatment', all films are adaptations. Do we want to be 'just making pictures', as Stahr explains patronizingly to Boxley, or have we something larger in mind? Despite the conventional wisdom, it's noticeable how many of the best films are literary adaptations, like *The Last Tycoon* itself, never a big hit, with Robert De Niro as Stahr, Ingrid Boulting as Kathleen and Jack Nicholson as a Communist union organizer (this is the 1930s): cameras chasing cameras once again. Best to work from the best — from the Fieldings, Brontës, Tolstoys, Fitzgeralds indeed — and leave some wiggle room for 'amateurism', humility, imperfection. Not everything need be perfectly done and dusted; not everything need fit into the digital chocolate box. Remember Brecht's 'alienation effect'? A continuity glitch, a raindrop on the lens: so what? It's only a bloody film. When we finally tire of the medium if we ever do (we're still, happily, not finished with traditional fine art) some ageing film libraries and a few books will remain, including histories of cinema and old editions of *Time Out Film Guide*. Cinema was a 20th-century thing, increasingly archaic now as life itself becomes a moving picture, a reality show in which everyone stars. As for those old theatrical releases, we can look back on them with amused nostalgia, as we do at the Regals and Odeons where we saw them for the first time. What fun it was then, going to the pictures!

Changing a Word

Heaney, laughing at me, would say, 'Why do you only write *great* poems?' And I'd laugh back, 'Sure you're only a great poet yourself.' But I knew what he meant. The unborn child, the disused shed: 'award-winning' items both perhaps, not 'great' either of them but each written in an old-fashioned rhetorical mode which seems to claim too much: a bit presumptuous for a twenty-year-old undergraduate ('An Unborn Child'), and a bit pompous ('A Disused Shed') for a slow-to-develop thirty-year-old. I've been looking at them again. Changing a word after many years is risky, even riskier changing a phrase or a line; riskier still to rewrite a whole poem. (If only one could change the past, so open to tendentious misrepresentation.) But an unborn child doesn't batter, it kicks; and the world doesn't waltz, it revolves. The mother in the first of these was Wendy, wife of dashing Grattan Puxon, an activist in the 'Itinerant' cause; they lived in a mews cottage, long since demolished, off Lower Mount St., Dublin, in the early 1960s. The scene there was simple as in the poem: the kitten, the goldfish bowl, the bulb, the sewing. I thought I was being clever with the theatrical 'rehearse' and 'produce', the title of the Susan Hayward film, *I Want to Live!* (1958) and the allusion to 'protest'. (We did a lot of protesting and demonstrating in those days.) But other things were going on that I didn't notice at the time; for the poem, by a very young man, is in a sense autobiographical: like a child I hadn't yet faced the world and its 'splitting light'. This light, I see, shines again in the disused shed ten years later. Both poems take place in semi-darkness; both hope for illumination and activity, for life indeed, and in both the light is a restricted one though none the less intense for that. My mushrooms, straining towards the keyhole, aren't real mushrooms, for real mushrooms don't behave like that, and in extenuation I can only plead poetic licence. It's a very derivative piece of work. The basic premise derives from J. G. Farrell (see 'Huts and Sheds' in *Selected Prose*); the 'powdery prisoners' are remembered from an old film of Charles Dickens' *A Tale of Two Cities*, and the triffids come from John Wyndham. The 'waltzing' world was suggested by Kubrick's use of a Blue Danube theme in his space movie *2001* (1968). A change from 'waltzing' to 'revolving' loses that derivative filmic gesture and admits (r)evolution into the scheme of things. So much more interesting than a kitschy waltz; or is dance better than history?

The great Joseph Joubert (1754-1824) speaks of 'words agreeable to the eye, in the same way that there are words agreeable to the ear, by a fortunate combination of the letters that form them or by the harmony of those letters, for each letter has its shape' (tr. Paul Auster). This plays a part in the choice or change of a word. 'Batter' isn't particularly agreeable to the eye; 'kick' is, though, with its graphic *k*'s. 'Waltz' is vivid, and a *z* is always fun, but the proximity to 'schmaltz' is problematic. 'Revolve' is agreeable to eye, ear and hand; it looks, sounds and *feels* like what it means, like its near synonym 'rotate'. And so on. Lines may need revising. 'A Bangor Requiem', for instance, moved awkwardly at first, and I felt a need to be more inclusive, to make this an elegy not only for my mother but for a community of 'friends and relatives, declining too'. As for the rewriting of an entire poem, this was the case with 'Lapis Lazuli', so loquacious and even gabbling in its first version; it needed tightening up. So a fifty-line gabble shrank to twenty-one lines, three stanzas of seven lines each. Harry Clifton, to whom the poem is dedicated, had his doubts about this, but even personal considerations are overridden by aesthetic compulsion, so he'll have to put up with it. Sorry, Harry; and sorry too if you're sometimes eerily confused with the Harry Clifton of Yeats's 'Lapis Lazuli' to which my poem refers. Geology aside, my paperweight, 'uncut and knobbly as a meteorite', a present from the sculptor Fleur Fitzgerald, bears no resemblance to the incised stone your namesake gave to our great predecessor.

This from *Edward* Fitzgerald's *Rubáiyát of Omar Khayyám*

(remember him, the jug of wine etc?):

> *The moving finger writes and, having writ,*
> *Moves on; not all thy piety nor wit*
> *Shall lure it back to cancel half a line*
> *Nor all thy tears wash out a word of it.*

Tears? Howls, more like, so frightful can be the experience of re-reading your early stuff. As we grow older the idiocies and ineptitudes of youthful work become increasingly obvious. We blush at our juvenilia, and even at later things put down at an age when we should have known better; and this applies to private correspondence too, for everything ends up in archive libraries, to be scrutinized, and perhaps misinterpreted, by not always friendly eyes. You can still get a good price there for a soul, but it's like anything else in life, we regret our past performance and want to set things right if we can; mostly we can't. We can never unwrite a thing in print — but new editions, if we're fortunate enough to run to new editions, provide opportunities for revision. At least for some of us nothing is ever finished; the most we can hope for is a proximate finality — a work, or a group of works, in something like final shape, representing the best we can do with our material. So Kavanagh's dire projection becomes the new creativity:

> *Correct the proofs over and over,*
> *Rewrite old poems again and again.*
>   ('To Be Dead')

There's little we can do about posterity except make some slight provision in the form of a few decent pages. Many poets, perhaps superstitious about revision, have chosen to leave things as they are, though they might reasonably have done otherwise. Setting aside the extreme case of Auden, some of the outstanding 20th-century poets could have dropped or rewritten much of their work with benefit to themselves and us. MacNeice and Lowell come to mind. However admirable its intentions we could have managed perfectly well without MacNeice's *Ten Burnt Offerings*;

and Lowell's unworked later 'sonnet' books — *History, For Lizzie and Harriet, The Dolphin* — have positively the air of an imposition, doing nothing for his reputation then or since. Some write as if everything they commit to paper is worthy of publication. Our sloppier stuff may be of minor interest but it interferes with what we like to consider the real thing.

In 'our line of work' (Brodsky's phrase), as in any other, it's important to distinguish the bad from the not-so-bad, to recognize the falsities and failures. Hostile critics, oneself among them, will occasionally suggest that the whole life's work is a failure, to which Beckett gave the answer: 'Try again. Fail again. Fail better.' Besides, failure has its uses. It instils humility and keeps you young; internalized, a habit of thought, it makes you tentative and contrarian, a rare and valuable combination in the 'real world' of bond markets and infotech. It keeps you on the edge, the 'cutting' edge, though you won't so much *cut* in that sense as ruminate, reflect. Since disinterested reflection is frowned upon by the banks, and now by the universities, you find yourself in an enviable position on the outside, looking in. Who could ask for anything more? You can spend days changing a line, a phrase, a word, to the cries of seagulls. Your failures have no importance there; 'failure' itself means nothing. The great danger is solipsism; personal failure is of little consequence in light of the larger historic failures — though these too have their use in reminding us of our evidently unchanging nature and situation. Some of the greats were failures as the world understands the term: Coleridge, Baudelaire, and Kafka who said: 'One must cheat no one, not even the world of its triumph.' Acceptance of worldly failure exempts you from the rat race and leaves you in peace to think about more important things. Revision is about past failures — failures of inspiration and expertise, and also the personal failure. We rehabilitate ourselves in language; to change a word or a line is to tweak the soul. Not only readers but writers too can revise and perhaps 'improve' themselves through poetry. 'To thine own self be true'? Yes, but what if the self is in serious need of revision?

Prose often needs revising too. Developments in the public sphere, at home and abroad, are soon history. Authors you've written about publish new work; you change your mind about things or acquire new perspectives. Something too quick, too 'journalistic' in the bad sense, will need to be replaced. I keep changing not only poems but also bits of prose that still seem to matter; the poetic fidgets are at work here too. Besides obvious typos ('ration' for 'ratio') due to my own hasty proof-reading, besides factual errors and the like, some things seem inadequate in retrospect and need a little adjustment. The J. G. Farrell material in *Selected Prose*, for example, needs tightening up and a better sense of the back story, the 'influences'. (I'm not the first Farrellite to notice the ghosts of *Gormenghast, The Leopard* and *Cold Comfort Farm*, of *The Plague* and *Vanity Fair*.) Oddly, despite some journalistic experience I often read prose — my own and others' — like verse, and write it too with a verse rhythm in mind. I even catch me inditing sentences that behave a bit like iambic pentameters, 'and wríte them tóo with a vérse rhýthm in mínd', if you see what I mean. I'm not talking about 'poetic' prose, God forbid; the very thought is so pretentious. Yes, but on consideration there's something to be said for the pretentious. It can be fun; it can open up new perspectives. Aren't some of the great things shamelessly pretentious? Don't want to go too far in that direction; and these bits and pieces aren't great things by any means, but often merely overgrown book reviews: a dying art.

Rubbish Theory

We hear of a sea of rubbish, hundreds of miles wide, in the Pacific. Inquire further and you find this is only one of several in the oceans, albeit the largest, and is actually composed of two, the interacting East and West Pacific Gyres that combine to make up the Great Pacific Garbage Patch north of Hawaii. It sounds benign, like 'cabbage patch', but is quite the opposite. Rotating slowly in a clockwise direction, it draws in plastics since these aren't biodegradable; the rest sinks to the sea floor to join an even bigger, underwater rubbish dump. Most of this debris comes from land-based activities, the rest from shipping and offshore oil rigs. Non-biodegradable but *photo*degradable, plastics are reduced by sunlight and gradually break down into tiny pieces resembling marine organisms, often mistaken for food by birds and fish. When they swallow these non-nutrients they swallow, too, toxic chemicals the plastic has absorbed, and these enter the food chain. The size of the zone is hard to determine since the plastic broth isn't evident from the air, but estimates range from an area the size of Texas to ten percent of the entire Pacific Ocean, says the *National Geographic*; and drones have found there's a hundred times more plastic by weight than previously realized. The Gyre is too large for scientists to 'trawl'; and who's going to clean it up? The US? Japan? The UN? Some other, dedicated international organization? 'Scientists and explorers agree that limiting or eliminating the use of disposable plastics and increasing the use of biodegradable resources will be the best way to solve the problem.' They also estimate it would take seventy ships a year to clean up one percent of the North Pacific, so we're not going to see real results any time soon; though there's a Dutch scheme at the development stage which may prove to be the answer.

Meanwhile the pictures tell the story: turtles and seals entangled in cast-off plastic nets; dead seabirds, their exposed stomachs choked with gas lighters and bottle caps.

The more stuff we produce the more rubbish there is to dispose of, from yoghurt cartons to nuclear waste. Some things — domestic kitsch, tourist tat — are rubbish from their point of manufacture, others victims of built-in obsolescence. The inhabited world is filled with junk, much of it for sale, even more of it for disposal; increasingly, junk orbits in space. These things are either tributes to recent 'growth', symptoms of self-defeating consumerist disregard, or both; but the litter mounts up, the skips are persistently full to overflowing. 'In an ideal world,' said Michael Thompson in his ground-breaking *Rubbish Theory* (Oxford, 1979), 'an object would reach zero value and zero expected life-span at the same instant, and then . . . disappear into dust. But, in reality, it doesn't do this; it just continues to exist in a timeless and valueless limbo where, at some later date (if it has not by that time turned, or been made, into dust) it has the chance of being discovered.' *Rubbish Theory* has much to recommend it; but Thompson's parameters derive from the world of market research (antiques etc) and he overlooks the significance of dust. He's talking about old lamps and furniture, the things that can play a role in gentrification, not the household and industrial waste whose working lives are presumed to be at an end; whose limbo is the dump. So, is that the last of them? Do the scrap metal and broken glass disappear into earth and air, an irrelevant residue not to be seen again? No, they've an active future, and even used plastic can be moulded into bricks. Meanwhile the environmental degradation continues: naff advertising, daft architecture, wobbly bridges, ugly apartment houses barely fit for purpose, torture music, moronic interventions in public space — a bench with a plaque reading 'Everybody needs a place to think' (nobody sits there), another bench with a sculpture of two grannies in conversation and no room for real grannies; the crumpled cans, the styrofoam. On the home front, however, much improvement. New, smart bins, no longer inanimate objects, have joined the 'internet of things', report back to their owners when they're full, and provide remote monitoring systems for the waste and recycling industries.

I had it written out for me as if for an imbecile: clean paper, cardboard, plastic and tin cans to recycling; food waste to the compost heap; other waste to the incineration bin; ashes to ashes, dust to dust. The first category takes up most space since it includes newspapers and packaging. Recycling, in one form or another, has always been with us; traditional Hinduism even gives the individual soul a series of different lives. (Please, next time, can I be a maharajah?) Revolutions help; also wars, I'm afraid. Thomas Pynchon, writing of wartime England in *Gravity's Rainbow* (1973), a hard-to-read but sometimes startlingly poetic cult book in its day, imagines 'thousands of old used toothpaste tubes in the pipefitters' sheds, heaped often to the ceilings', which are 'returned to the war, heaps of dimly fragrant metal, phantoms of peppermint in the winter shacks, each tube wrinkled by the unconscious hands of London, written over in interference patterns, hand against hand, waiting now . . . to be melted for solder, for plate, alloyed for castings, bearings, gasketry, hidden smoke-shriek linings the children of that other domestic incarnation will never see'. But children love rubbish, both for its own sake and even sometimes for profit: the stuff in their bags and pockets, the copper wire from clapped-out, dumped computers. Besides, living closer to ground level, they're more conscious of debris and rejectamenta, the scrunched tin-foil and the grapefruit rind. Amateurs, *cognoscenti* of rags, bones and discarded bubble wrap, they live in a world of secret expertise. All ladders start, for Yeats, in 'the foul rag-and-bone shop of the heart'; and Brecht advised, 'Don't start with the good old things, start with the bad new ones.'

Whatever about the good old things there are certainly plenty of bad new ones: bad books, bad art, bad music in abundance, the lot validated by post-modern dumbing down — and let's not forget 'upcycled' Rubbish Art. There's rubbish and rubbish, the literal (dust and ashes, rags and bones) and the metaphorical: the bad books and art which become literal rubbish too as they crumble away in their black holes — though the abject object, if not destined for oblivion, can have a retro mystique and even an artistic aura. I myself tried to capture this in 'A Garage in Co. Cork'. The poem, says Hugh Haughton, is 'about a site of exhausted modernity, though cluttered with "intact antiquities of the recent past" . . . not vestiges of traditional Ireland, but an obsolete filling station surrounded by a detritus of soft-drink ads and scrap iron. [The poem] reflects on it through the lens of Michael Thompson whose *Rubbish Theory* offered an account of the changing status of mass-produced goods as they moved from the retail catalogue to rubbish to being collectables, and from "transients" to "durables", in a cycle where they start and end as valuable aesthetic objects but pass through a stage of being junk.'

What concerns me here is the evidently *unsalvageable* junk, the forlorn things with no hope of ever being antiques or even relics of contemporary material culture: not the old toys and utensils but the organic stuff, the rags and bones destined for toxic incineration or for tips hazy with methane and loud with screaming gulls. The discarded stuff lives on though; there's a dark energy there in the dustbins of history, of potential use in some future ecological dispensation. Nothing is ever completely lost, energy can't be destroyed but only changed from one form to another: 'If you want me again look for me under your boot-soles' (Whitman, 'Song of Myself'). As we know, everything in nature goes round and round — including ourselves. We perpetuate ourselves in our children; and, buried or dispersed, mutate over time into vegetation like figures from Ovid. Can we read the *Metamorphoses* as an extended metaphor of species evolution? The most remarkable developments take place. As people in Ovid change into plants and birds, and ivory into human flesh, so too, perhaps over generations, the disadvantaged can often translate themselves into other, 'superior' life forms, to inherit the earth one day. *Nei rifiuti del mondo nasce un nuovo mondo*, says Pasolini: 'In the refuse of the world a new world is born.' His new world is not, in fact, a salubrious one, but the axiom is so perfect it can stand alone, even if the *rifiuti* are problematic. Does he mean things, people, or both? If people, the designation is harsh, like 'scum of the earth', though not quite so contemptuous. He himself, knifed to death on waste ground, finished up in the refuse (a bird-like sculpture marks the spot);

but the future hides in the dust and ashes, awaiting its moment.

James Cameron (*An Indian Summer*, 1974) describes a Madras room-sweeper going through the motions of cleaning a floor. He's not really cleaning the floor, but he has to show dedication for the sake of his job: 'He must be abased and silent, yet somehow evident, careful never to raise his eyes, squatting crabwise around the room among the dust which is his livelihood and which therefore must be identified with, stirred and agitated and shifted from one place to another . . . He fulfilled the role society required of him merely by associating himself as nearly as he could with the dirt in which he dealt; his efficiency was of minor importance. A vacuum cleaner would work better, but it would cost more.' This isn't really patronizing. The sweeper, perhaps a maharajah now, or an infotech tycoon, owing to his dutiful humility in that former life, can congratulate himself on the workings of *karma* — though he'd need to watch his step or he'll be back there in the dust the next time round. The *karma* principle, that of reincarnation, of existential recycling, works both ways. The bat may have been a politician once, the rat a banker, which it probably was. (Be afraid, be very afraid.) Conversely, a virtuous fly may take human form.

Grown-ups, except for those who have no choice, prefer to ignore rubbish or even deny its existence. Cameron again: 'Indians of all varieties . . . will promenade through streets of almost indescribable filth, littered with refuse and debris, gutters adrift with ordure, picking their way through the muck with a skilfully intuitive indifference, since *they do not see it*. Themselves in their persons they are clean; all else is maya, illusion.' A stray child though, in India or anywhere else, might loiter in a trance among the trash, intrigued by the environmental degradation, bewitched by a dead transistor in a ditch or an old bike in a stream, frozen for ten minutes in mute rapture before running home. This kind of fascination is shared by contemplative adults like David Gascoyne who, in his poem 'The Gravel-Pit Field' (1941), catches a glimpse of the field's philosophical and even religious implications. It's littered with all sorts of rubbish, but in a shaft of sunlight, in 'a last lucidity of day', he sees its 'apotheosis':

> *No-man's-land*
> *Between this world and the beyond,*
> *Remote from men and yet more real*
> *Than any human dwelling-place;*
> *A tabernacle where one stands*
> *As though within the empty space*
> *Round which revolves the Sage's Wheel.*

The apotheosis of rubbish! There's now an aesthetics of trash; thing theory posits 'soul' in inanimate matter; redemption of the disregarded and marginalized may yet extend to the waste paper and the banana skin. The *rifiuti*, in due course, will have their time in the sun.

Clouds

Hide; hide, and keep an eye on the global spies, the eyes in the
sky who have their eyes on *you*. They know where you live and
what you think, and their knowledge . . . no, their information,
or misinformation, represents a sort of power. They can pick you
off whenever they please, or so they may imagine, like a Texas-
based 'biographer' who had me in his sights a while ago or
thought he had — his war aim, I surmise, to take out a tiny
pocket of resistance to the imperium. (A trashy, twisted piece of
work, not serious; but y'know, the worse the book the better in
cases like that.) Some of us recognize an older and larger know-
ledge, cloud wisdom you might say, the authority of the indeter-
minate — though even clouds have been enlisted in the present
snoopy age. Modern cloud science began with Luke Howard
(1772-1864), the original cloud computer, an English Quaker,
who published in *The Philosophical Magazine* a widely noted
essay, 'On the Modifications of Clouds' (1803): see Richard
Hamblyn, *The Invention of Clouds*, 2001. Howard drew atten-
tion to cloud species and varieties, named and numbered these
(hence 'Cloud Nine') and tried to recognize some order in the
nubilous chaos. 'Nubilous' was Constable's word. A Howard
fan, he was doing his Hampstead Heath cloud studies just a few
years later; art and science drew closer during the Romantic era.
But cloud thoughts have been going on since ancient times and
still do. We ever been *inside* clouds for example? Sure we have, on
high hills or in flight when, coming in to land, we descend from
the ether through cumulus white and dark, through rain clouds,
the plane windows streaming with condensation, before bump-
ing down to earth. 'Sublime' and 'beautiful' both, in the time-
honoured philosophical terms — tumultuous or sedative — they
answer in their own good time to every psychic need. Clouds in

Irish landscape art? Always there, or never far away, since J. A. O'Connor — special mention going to Paul Henry and to Nathaniel Hone's north Co. Dublin skies.

Aristophanes, satirizing Socratic sophistry, introduced (420 BC) 'the celestial Clouds, tutelary goddesses of the layabout, from whom come our intelligence, dialectic and reason, our speculative genius and argumentative talents'. Lucretius, in *The Nature of Things*, describes the cloud contribution at length. *De Rerum Natura*, Bk.6.441 *ff*.: 'Clouds mass together, when in the space of the sky above a large number of flying bodies have come together in mutual attachment. These first cause small clouds to be formed; then these take hold and cluster together', and so on in the obviously reliable if slightly boring Loeb idiom. Lucretius' text, in the nature of things, asks for a *verse* translation:

> *Clouds take shape in the blue skies and gather*
> *where flying bodies get tangled up together;*
> *and tiny clouds are blown along by breezes*
> *till the moment when a stronger current rises . . .*

Cloud writers of later vintage (Shakespeare, Coleridge, Baudelaire, Yeats, Stevens) are many, none more observant than the Coleridge of the *Notebooks*: 'Slanting pillars of misty light moved along under the sun hid by clouds.' None more vigorous than Yeats, one of the most distinguished citizens — a Senator indeed — of Cloud-cuckooland, the Aristophanic dream world we still inhabit today. He was sparing but forceful in his use of clouds, one aspect of his Celtic-twilit relish for dramatic weather conditions: 'The wind has bundled up the clouds high over Knocknarea'; 'this tumult in the clouds' (the 'Irish Airman'). Clouds are always there in Yeats even when not specifically mentioned. They *are* specifically mentioned in 'The Tower', when in his early sixties he already saw himself as an old man (how times have changed!): 'It is time that I wrote my will'; 'Now shall I make my soul'. As we get older the poets of senescence, once barely credible, become personally relevant —

like Yeats himself whose own 'decrepitude' and the death of friends, among them admired women, begin to lose focus and meaning:

> *Seem but the clouds of the sky*
> *When the horizon fades;*
> *Or a bird's sleepy cry*
> *Among the deepening shades.*

He would use 'shade' to mean not only shadow but ghost, as in 'To a Shade' (Parnell). A bit dyslexic, let's say hasty, even so he knew exactly what he was doing with the punctuation here. The semi-colon after 'fades' has, I think, a special point. If it were only a comma, the lines would mean just what they say, no more nor less — but the semi-colon anticipates something more poignant to come; for he takes his place here among the deepening 'shades' of his own historical phase. He is himself cloud, bird and shade, and the poem is his own sleepy cry.

Unlike Goethe for instance (remember Goethe?), who delighted in Howard's scientific approach and even wrote poems about it, Yeats belonged to what we might call the indeterminate school. He wouldn't have been interested in the categorizing of clouds; for him, as for most of us, the whole point of them is that they're vague and unpredictable. Nature itself insists on this sort of thing: there has to be elbow room, wiggle room, one reason for art, for poetry indeed, and one of the consolations of decrepitude. The clouds of the sky, in their vague way, evade human thought, even while inspiring it, preferring to leave themselves open (camel, weasel, 'very like a whale') to whimsical interpretation or its absence; like life, unless we take a religious view, they mean nothing but themselves or how we decide to think of them: 'To make the shifting clouds be what you please' (Coleridge). Can't seem to put my hand on the cloud notes I used to keep, but that's appropriate enough. Clouds, after all, can't be relied upon, wherein lies their enduring fascination. Wind and water, who'd have thought they could be commodified and 'privatized'? But now they are. Clouds are trickier: they seem, in the nature of things, unmindful of market forces. So let's celebrate clouds, their vagueness and inconsequence; and old age too, when their real significance, or insignificance, take on their final existential roles (*The Tempest*, IV. 1.152 *ff.*):

> *The cloud-capped towers, the gorgeous palaces,*
> *The solemn temples, the great globe itself,*
> *Yea, all which it inherit, shall dissolve*
> *And, like this insubstantial pageant faded,*
> *Leave not a rack behind. We are such stuff*
> *As dreams are made on, and our little life*
> *Is rounded with a sleep. Sir, I am vext.*
> *Bear with my weakness; my old brain is troubled.*

Editions of the play note that a 'rack' was a shred of cloud, and the Penguin adds: 'The word also had a technical application to the stage clouds often used in court masques to dissolve a scene. This secondary meaning reinforces the underlying sense in Prospero's description of the dissolution of the world as being like that of some great court performance.' There are puns and echoes here in this famous speech, 'rack' and 'wrack' (wreck) for example, and even perhaps a presage of ecological disaster. A strange fate for the species, to leave not a wrack behind in the drowned world, though it's not as if we haven't been warned: 'Yond same cloud cannot choose but fall by pailfuls' (Trinculo).

Cloud notes
— Camões' Adamastor, Cape of Storms (Good Hope), a symbolic cloud shape blacking out the sky: 'a monstrous, fearsome thing' (tr. W. C. Atkinson) representing nature at its most fierce and warning of violent retribution for human presumption in broaching 'unknown' regions of the earth.
— Sun's eye peeping from behind clouds, an ideogram for speakeasy or perhaps espionage; moon-dashing 'rapid' clouds like cannon smoke as in Larkin's poem 'Sad Steps'.
— iCloud, a cloud bank, as if we hadn't enough banks already.

— Nephology, infotech, convection. Why didn't I get a real scientific education at Kelvin's old school?

— 'I do set my bow in the cloud, and it shall be for a token of a covenant between me and the earth' (Genesis 9:13).

— 'Thought forms in the soul as clouds form in the air' (Joubert).

Responsibilities begin in dreams, and Stevens was the great cloud dreamer of modern times, if too luxurious for some tastes. A conservative and an intensely private man, his responsibilities seem, at first glance, confined to domestic and business life in Hartford; but the poems tell a more expansive story. Even, or especially, his more euphoric, more *literal* vapourings illustrate a grand responsibility to art as a way of life and thought. 'The Idea of Order at Key West', with its almost physical Muse-evocation, is the great instance. There are 'bronze shadows' here, 'high horizons', no clouds specifically but they're there: those 'bronze shadows'. Elsewhere we have 'the speech of clouds' (his own practice surely), 'the sea unfolding in the sunken clouds' in that November off Tehuantepec and, in 'Notes Toward a Supreme Fiction', 'the top-cloud of a May night-evening', 'frothy' clouds like waves, and a cloud angel obviously related to her nibs at Key West. He notes, in 'An Ordinary Evening in New Haven', 'the difference that clouds make over a town'. America has its own kinds of reality, and its own ways of seeing; but I think here of European things like, for example, Aelbert Cuyp's 17th-century views of Dordrecht beneath puffy-cheeked, driven cumulus, its glowing billows almost forming human, or perhaps angelic, faces. If Pound was 'really' a sculptor and Eliot a musician, Stevens was really a painter; and indeed he had quite a collection.

We get a lot of clouds down here in Kinsale — cirrus, stratus, cumulus, even night-shining clouds; but especially, slashed by high vapour trails, the cumulus that gathers on these southern shores as if flown in each morning directly from Bermuda, and maybe it is. Up north, along the Derry and Antrim coasts for example, the heart quails at the violent, as it were apocalyptic contrast between earth and sky: such tiny houses, such enormous clouds! Down here it's milder, more domesticated, more beautiful than sublime; but vast fleecy flocks, surprising as Aristophanes' cloud chorus, are often framed in my desk window as if to establish a context: perfect working conditions except that they're so distracting. They move slowly and tactfully, giving time for reflection on this and that, chiefly their own metaphorical implications. A standing, drifting reproach to organization and number, to the monetarization of life and the rule of system, they are the great alternative. Hamblyn quotes Goldsmith (remember Goldsmith?): 'Every cloud that moves, and every shower that falls, serves to mortify the philosopher's pride, and to show him hidden qualities in air and water that he finds difficult to explain.' They *are* explicable of course, as the 'philosopher', the natural scientist Howard demonstrated; but, while fully aware of the meteorology, we still like to think of them as mysterious. We need the indeterminate things, like love and poetry, that seem to resist a too rational explanation. Bachelard, in *L'Air et les songes* ('Air and Daydreams'), is a bit severe about the 'oneiric' character of cloud reverie which, he says, is without responsibility. He cites Éluard and others to the effect that, while providing dream alternatives to harsh reality, cloud consolations are 'facile and ephemeral'; reality, harsh or not, is what we have to deal with. But clouds are real too; each one, like life itself, is ephemeral but substantial, from the pale fluff to the dark turmoil. Our ephemeral lives, like 'the clouds of the sky', are no less real for being ephemeral. Are cloud thoughts without consequence? Responsibilities, after all, begin in dreams.

School Photo and Early Reading

There was a time when I couldn't have studied a thing like this in detail without prescription lenses, but now I can. (Eyes, it seems, like brains, can *improve* with age.) I look first at the background. Old brick, windows reflecting trees in the enclosed play area — chestnuts, I seem to remember, so many shiny conkers bursting out of their prickly skins: Skegoneil Primary School in the late 1940s, then at the bottom of the Old Cavehill Road, later moved and replaced by a local library; and now . . . ? There was a sweetshop on the corner — Liquorice Allsorts, Dolly Mixtures — suddenly crowded on the day post-war rationing came to an end. Miss Young wore a yellow blouse with a cameo brooch at the throat; Miss Kane stood at the top of the stairs at break time wagging a finger, repeating 'Walk, don't run' to the swarming infants. And here in the black-and-white photo are some of us, thirty or so, in four ascending rows: my own crowd, the front rows seated on folding chairs, the back rows standing on benches, watching the camera lens with its black hood, the wee old faces already somehow foreshadowing future lives. Denis Deacon and Linda Farrell, where are you now? Jim Morrow, Sheila Shannon? Deirdres and Trevors, Brians and Annes. Here's the chap with whom I started saving up for a yacht to sail to the West Indies (we lost interest); and there's a bad boy, surly and wild, born to be hanged you would say, who ran in front of a tram and broke a leg. There's the girl I liked best but who didn't like me particularly, and another whose beauty and keen good nature are evident already: a lovely smile. Some of the bigger girls look quite mumsy, some of the boys like promising citizens, some tough. There are boys clearly destined for the rugger field and resolute careers. Girls and boys both are grinning or giggly, serious, shy, and some, like me, of doubtful significance; but all, or most, have *character* of an old-fashioned kind. Short trousers, knees, pullovers, tartan skirts, hair ribbons, fringes, partings; Clarks sandals (pull up your socks). Social classes, working and middle: a toff here, a rough diamond there, but all equal in childhood. Protestant-reared of course, their parents Unionist voters. Our Westminster MP (Belfast North) was H. Montgomery Hyde — barrister, author — who, though a Unionist, later urged the return of the Lane pictures to Dublin and was put out of the party. I've just re-read his very fair-minded book about the trial of Roger Casement.

Home reading in the Skegoneil years included the usual comics and annuals, and obvious things like the William books, Enid Blyton, illustrated editions of *Crusoe, Treasure Island* and *Tom Sawyer* — anything really, preferably with 'pictures and conversations'. My mother disliked William (those dirty clothes), but I adopted him as a role model, though really he was a bit of a bore. Blyton's 'famous five' kept me going for months at a certain stage; but, looking again at *Five Go to Smuggler's Top*, I can see she was a bad writer, prolific and lazy at the same time — though tomboy George was interesting. Tom Sawyer, another version of William, was a good lad, especially when he and Becky Thatcher got lost in McDougal's Cave: very touching, that. A precocious reading of Kipling's *Captains Courageous* bothered me greatly. It seemed a good yarn but also baffling. How come, for example, the Portuguese fishermen's home port was Gloucester, an inland town in England surely? (Only on re-reading it years later did I realize it was Gloucester, Massachusetts, with its Portuguese community.) The other Kipling in my life, *The Jungle Book*, provided the pre-Boy Scout mythology behind the 'Wolf Cubs'. I rose through the ranks but later, bored with the Scouts, quit and followed my mates into the school (Inst) cadet corps — which meant, among other things, an occasional rifle practice, aiming .22s at distant targets on a range. Seán Haldane and others did fine, but I was no use at all since the targets were continually out of focus — whence perhaps a lifelong dislike of guns. I continued playing soldiers under the eye of an ex-sergeant of the Royal Ulster Rifles, but my heart wasn't in it. What I really fancied was a deck apprenticeship in the Merchant Navy, about which I went on and on. To shut me up my father took me for a physical to a Ministry of Transport doctor down the docks. The first thing was the eyesight test, which proved to be the last thing too. Read off the chart, said the doc: GTQX etc. What chart, said I; and that was the end of my seagoing dream. Corrective specs soon followed, so I'd a kind of goggles for reading Biggles, *in toto*, and my favourite book at the time, an abridged version of Nicholas Monsarrat's *The Cruel Sea* (1951), about the wartime Battle of the Atlantic.

Specs. There's a scene in one of Woody Allen's films where a blocked writer (Woody) is briefly visited by the Muse, very like Miss Kane, a no-nonsense young woman in a white robe and angel wings, who gives him a brisk talking-to. She holds a quill pen and a parchment, and wears heavy horn-rimmed specs as if to emphasize her serious purpose; and isn't there a girl with specs in one of the William books? None of those in the Skegoneil photo is wearing specs. No doubt some are wearing them now, or have had laser treatment, and probably some are dead; but two died even then. A bespectacled boy, not in the photo, was carried off by a chest infection; and a girl, dashing into the Antrim Road, was struck by a car and killed. The deaths of the very young! . . . We won't meet them in heaven (why not?), says the American poet Donald Justice, but:

> *If anywhere, in the deserted schoolyard at twilight*
> *Forming a ring, perhaps, or joining hands*
> *In games whose very names we have forgotten.*
> ('On the Death of Friends in Childhood')

Real grown-up reading began in adolescence. The old Smithfield covered market, with its second-hand books, wasn't far from Inst, so I'd often linger there on my way home, picking up for a shilling or two *Great Expectations, Sons and Lovers* and a short-ened version of *Moby-Dick*; also, intrigued by the startling pictures, Eileen O'Faoláin's *Irish Sagas and Folk-Tales* (1954) — an eye-opener. Huxley's early novels seemed clever things to have, but I couldn't get my head around them then. Same with Joyce's *Dubliners*, which I tried too soon. Prescribed texts included Shakespeare plays and *A Pageant of English Verse*: Pope, Keats, Hopkins. In French we did part one of Alain-Fournier's *Le Grand Meaulnes*. Locals, not prescribed: Forrest Reid and Louis MacNeice, Rodgers and Hewitt. I was given Inst's Forrest Reid composition prize (he was an Old Boy), which proved to be a copy of his *Retrospective Adventures* (1941), and opened his *Peter Waring* too, though without much enthusiasm: Patricia Craig, in *Bookworm* ('A Memoir of Childhood Reading'), remarks on his lack of 'vivacity'. On the other hand, she says, 'there *is* that tenderness for landscape and animals and friendship'; but rough youth is impatient with that sort of thing.

We weren't impatient with 'The Big Moan', though perhaps we should have been. We admired those older boys (it was a boys' school) who had already acquired girlfriends, and Augustin Meaulnes was a prototype of these. The story, you remember, is related by François Seurel, like Fournier the son of a country schoolmaster. It tells how Meaulnes, a strange moody boy of imposing aspect, arrives at the school and is hero-worshipped by his fellows including François himself, who becomes his friend and confidant. When Frank Davison's English translation (later re-issued as *The Lost Domain*) appeared very belatedly in 1959 I read on more rapidly (for the story) in the school library. Meaulnes, emotionally precocious, is fascinated by the daughter of a château some miles off. Together the two boys visit there after dark, finding the place *en fête*, and join the party. Meaulnes meets Yvonne, they fall in love, and eventually they marry. Older now, Meaulnes disappears to Paris on a mysterious errand during her difficult first pregnancy; she dies in childbirth. Later Meaulnes reappears and claims his child, reluctantly surrendered by its surrogate dad François, who is in love with *everybody*: 'Already I pictured him, in the night, wrapping his daughter in a cloak, to carry her off with him on some new adventure.' This is a brutally simplified outline of the book, which is rich in mysteries and nuances of all kinds, besides being a percipient study of schoolboy psychology and a classic figuration of what might be called the Gallic Twilight

— a theatrical property box it shares with Laforgue and many another: the distant piano, the sad clown. Its strength lies in its circumstantial realism: the snowy boots around the school-room stove, the phenol-soaked cotton wool in which Yvonne's dead body is wrapped: 'I like the marvellous,' said Fournier, 'only when it's strictly enveloped in reality.' Its weakness is its wild implausibility. Disqualified by its realism from the genre of fairy tale, it asks to be considered a grown-up book and judged as such.

The novelist J. G. Farrell, in an autobiographical piece, acknowledged a debt to Richard Hughes' *In Hazard*, first read as a child and again as an adult in the 'special state of narcosis' which comes with complete surrender to an authorial voice: 'The virtues of Hughes's writing, the relaxed tone, the hallucinating clarity of image, and the concreteness that gives substance to his vision, are qualities he shares with Conrad at his best.' Conrad was fine at short-story length but the novels were too much for me. Those narratives within narratives! I couldn't finish *Lord Jim*. It's one of the problems with adult fiction-reading in youth that you've no prior knowledge of the world being described, and no experience with which to measure events on the page; you breathe thin air and take it all on trust. With poetry it's different; you're breathing thin air anyhow and gladly believe anything. The young can have lots of fun with 'The Rape of the Lock' or the odes of Keats, but don't expose them to Henry James or Virginia Woolf: some knowledge of 'life' and of novelistic method are prerequisites. 'It seems to me now,' says Farrell, 'that it rained every day throughout my Irish adolescence . . . I sat at a streaming window reading Colette . . . And then one day, one year, it stopped raining at last, the clouds rolled away, and I stepped out into the watery sunlight of the real world, anxious to stop daydreaming and get on with it, whatever "it" might turn out to be.' My own teenage years were not so sheltered; I was already canning peas and hitching lifts on the Continent. When 'it' turned out to be an entrance scholarship from Trinity College, Dublin, I started reading — besides 'set books' — Beckett and other blithe, heartwarming modernists. As the great man put it in a note to Aidan Higgins, 'Despair early and never look back.' In hard times, to save expense and bother, he bought his wire-rimmed specs for a few francs at a flea market.

A Long Sunset

Olivia Manning, the author of *Fortunes of War*, had strong Ulster connections. Her mother, née Morrow, was a Bangor Presbyterian in origin; the family owned property in this largely Unionist town including a pub, the Old House at Home, in what is now High St. She married a Londoner, a naval lieutenant, and moved with him to Portsmouth where her daughter the novelist grew up; but there were regular visits back home, and Olivia went to school there during the first world war. Bangor appears in her first novel *The Wind Changes* (1937), where she calls it Carrickmoy. 'I come from the North,' says her heroine Elizabeth, an art student in Dublin: 'We lived at Carrickmoy. It's just where the coast turns the corner into Belfast Lough.' Manning continues, 'All the houses there faced the sea . . . In the winter the spray was flung over the roofs and flooded the back gardens . . . The salt nearly killed all the plants . . .' Kenneth Irvine quotes this at greater length in *The Bangor Book* (2016), which he edited, an anthology of 'Writing from and about Bangor and North Down'. Manning is the best-known modern writer cited, but he goes back much further — to 558 AD, in fact, when Comgall founded Bangor Abbey, where Columbanus also spent many years. The late Proinsias Mac Cana, of the Dublin Institute of Advanced Studies, calls it 'the cradle of Irish literature' on the strength of a rapid 6th-century extension of writing in Irish and 'an extraordinary quickening of artistic activity . . . The immediate sources of this were the scriptoria of certain monasteries', among which Bangor was prominent, and 'those monastic literati whom the metrical tracts refer to by the significant title of *nua litride*, "new men of letters"'. Of these Columbanus was one, though he left Bangor in due course to establish, famously, seminaries in France and Italy. His own writings, and codices like the Bangor Antiphonary, are key texts of the period and even provide fanciful descriptions of what the place was like in those early days. The Abbey declined in time and O'Neills acquired the land; but, with the failure of Con O'Neill's revolt against English rule, James I granted the lot to Sir James Hamilton of Clandeboye, from whom descend the Dufferins and others. The modern Bangor, wrote R. L. Praeger in 1947, 'with its bathing-pools and tennis clubs and buses and swarming motor cars, offers a strange contrast to the great religious establishment among its woods which the Northmen harried a thousand years ago'.

In the 'Writing Bangor' section Kenneth touches on Alice Milligan, who spent some of her early life there; John Hewitt, the same; William McQuitty, producer of the 1958 Titanic film *A Night to Remember*, who lived as a boy on the Princetown Road; Christopher FitzSimon, the theatre historian, who as a boy lived for a time on the Seacliff Road, as related in his memoir *Eleven Houses* (2007); and the novelist Charlotte Bingham, who lived as a girl in Bangor Castle, the family seat. Blackwoods, with Clandeboye connections, have long been active in the arts, and it was 19th-century Helen (Sheridan, Blackwood) Dufferin who wrote 'The Irish Emigrant', once a staple of popular anthologies, and gave her name to Helen's Bay. There are Bangor authors today, native or simply resident, but most Bangor writing seems to be about seaside holidays. Belfast names — Robert Harbinson, Rowel Friers, Gerald Dawe — make up the bulk of this material. 'God is Love', 'Jesus Saves': Harbinson notes the evangelical presence on Bangor's holiday beaches. Friers recalls the 'bathing boxes' (changing rooms), springboards and anchored raft for swimmers at Ballyholme, though not the donkey rides, and Dawe remembers the summer demographic, the extended families in rented houses: 'Bangor exerted an intimate and alluring hold on generations of ordinary Belfast people, long before cheap flights . . . I can still feel the excitement on stepping out of the railway station. Looking down Main St., I can still see the coal boats clanking, hear the gulls crying and imagine . . . all those men and women with their children, setting up temporary homes along the seafront. Grandfathers hobbling along . . . '

My own experience too. He namechecks Pickie Pool, no longer there, an open-air seawater baths at the west end of the promenade. (Who was Pickie? A local alderman?) Oh, I remember Pickie Pool with its *jeunesse dorée*, a clique of superior Princetown Rd.-style adolescents, five years or more my seniors, high-diving in rapid sequence as if they owned the place — as perhaps, in a sense, they did. A snap exists of a shy but delighted ten-year-old Derek (named, I think, for somebody 'on the wireless') at the wheel of a model jeep in a Bangor amusement arcade. This would have been 1950 or so, not long after 'the War'. Bangor had watched Allied warships rendezvous at the mouth of the lough prior to the D-Day landings, and some of the wartime buzz persisted for a few years; but that was grown-up stuff, dances and so on. Us youngsters were there for sea and sand, rocks and rock pools. An aunt had a house on the Seacliff Road which overlooked the frankly named 'Long Hole', a dark inlet abounding in submarine vegetation, and hours were spent there gazing into the water.

Ulster people in those days 'before cheap flights', cognizant of religious identity, took their holidays in different places: Donegal, South Down or the Antrim Glens for some, for others Bangor or Portrush. Louis MacNeice grew up on the Antrim side:

> *The brook ran yellow from the factory stinking of chlorine,*
> *The yarn-mill called its funeral cry at noon;*
> *Our lights looked over the lough to the lights of Bangor*
> *Under the peacock aura of a drowning moon.*
>
> ('Carrickfergus')

Did Bangor look romantic from Carrickfergus? It used to look quite romantic from Bangor too, by moonlight indeed or in stormy weather; but, like everywhere else, not enough care has been taken to save what it had of character, and it had quite a lot. Chainstore kitsch, with its idiot garish look, and civic procrastination of various kinds, have left parts of the town in an evidently permanent state of transience; though Bangor isn't alone in this. It's a global affliction. Bangor's just keeping up;

yet enough survives of Edwardian and inter-war style (now perhaps qualifying as venerable) to give a reassuring patina to residential neighbourhoods: the 'sunburst' gate, bay window, gravel, garage and rockery gardens. I've friends and cousins living there but I haven't been back for several years, when I stayed at the nice old Royal Hotel, now closed. The original railway station is long gone, and the new one looks like a shopping centre, but the 'baronial' Castle, now the Town Hall, is still in place; also Ward Park with its swans, peacocks and Big Gun, removed from a captured U-boat after the first world war and used by children since as a climbing frame. July was the holiday month when my one remaining granny would 'take a house' off Dufferin Avenue, ten minutes' walk (for me five minutes' run) from Pickie Pool. The house was dark, cramped and still gaslit in the fifties, but gaslight only added to the thrilling holiday atmosphere. I say my granny because this was when she came, briefly, into her own. With the old rip of a grandpa still at work in the Belfast shipyard, visiting only at weekends, she became the dominant figure and an outdoor one. Depending on the time of day she would sit, with a daughter or two in attendance, on a bench at the seafront or on the pier, to get the sun and receive old Belfast friends and acquaintances from her years in Duncairn Gardens and Seaview Parade. All this provided relief from her constant baking of soda bread on the griddle at home. Here, on the 'Twalfth', we would watch the Orangemen go by with their gloves, swords and blackthorn sticks, the fife-and-drum bands giving out 'The Sash' and 'Dolly's Brae' with forceful dedication. A 'great folk festival', sophisticated persons would concede. 'A great day', said everyone else.

My mother was buried at Clandeboye Cemetery; and next morning, a Sunday, I wandered off my usual course in search of a paper. This detour took me into Bangor West and I realized, from the names on commercial premises and the sight of a Catholic church, that this was a 'taig' neighbourhood, as the Twalfth men might have said, together with 'I've got nothing against them, but I wouldn't want to be ruled by them.' (There were also those, of course, who had plenty 'against them'.)

Mass was being sung in the church and shops were opening up; I might have been over the border in Carlingford or Bundoran. The quiet air of relaxation, the mild weather and sacred music, curiously suggestive of earlier times, composed a parallel, dozier town, the same but subtly different. Bangor is said to be eighty percent Protestant, but only eighty percent, though widely assumed to be close to 100%. To learn this, even late in life, was a relief: the thought of a solidly homogeneous population could be overwhelming, even alarming. And of course there are others too: Northern Ireland's second language, after all, is said to be not Irish but Chinese, or perhaps Polish. Ulster has yet to disclose its Chinese authors, but the 'Aspects' literary festival, created and run by Kenneth for many years, has hosted a comprehensive cast of Irish writers including the poets Montague, Heaney and Longley, the novelists J. P. Donleavy, Edna O'Brien and Jennifer Johnston, and a number of well-known academics and journalists. 'Aspects' has done much to dispel the undeservedly philistine reputation Bangor suffered for so long, which was really a form of snobbery: all those awful Belfast people with their ice-creams, the clock golf and the Bible cult, the raucous entertainment and bad taste. Yes, but what about the choirs and the first-rate Drama Club, cradle of several well-known professional actors?

Manning mentions the 'long sunsets' though these, as we know, are an Irish phenomenon and not unique to Bangor. But now there *is*, it must be said, a sunset quality to the place. I never could decide if that sunburst motif on gates and doors represents sun-up or sundown; but now it looks like sundown. With the Belfast crowd now taking their summer holidays abroad (direct flights from George Best City Airport), for Bangor as for other home resorts, here and elsewhere, the great days are over. Perhaps in time it will be again as it is in *The Wind Changes*: 'The big sandstone squares of the wall were weathered with hollows in which sea-water and rain-water collected. On the other side of the road were the tall, flat-fronted houses, grey, solid and upright against the gales. The shops had the casual, rather forsaken air of seaside shops. He thought it a dreary place.' Ah, but this is the situation, the cognitive zone, where art begins. I picture a daughter of Chinese immigrants standing there in the near future gazing out to sea, the first sentence of a story starting to form.

Here at the Grove

Crocuses, and other familiar species, I've known since my earliest years, from the Hineses' apple orchard next door off Salisbury Avenue, North Belfast; from Hazelwood farther out the Antrim Road and magical Gray's Lane bisecting the Fortwilliam golf course. I couldn't have definitely distinguished wood sorrel from wild garlic till much later; but here at the lovely Grove, known for its gardens, I've grown quite botanical in my old age, surrounded as I am by the flowers of the forest. It's just a flat in a house of holiday flats but it suits me fine, especially since the owners are so nice. I've never had a mortgage, never been on the property ladder; but here, where everyone seems to be on holiday the whole time, we have a 'grand', indeed rather *grand* set-up, with mature trees, outhouses and that sense of unique location, of special ambience, writers and artists find hard to resist. I don't know why it is, but somehow I've mostly lived in inviting places. I look back often and remember, for instance, Clifton Terrace, Monkstown, South Dublin; an attic on the west side of Fitzwilliam Square with its ivy and wrought-iron 'balconies', or the northwest corner of Washington Square when, between visits to the madhouse (a *real* education), I 'taught' in the New York university system. The Monkstown place was on the sea front but it was a garden flat, so instead of Howth across the bay we had a view of stone steps and the feet of descending guests, of whom there were many. Half a dozen of us lived there at different times, notably Eugene Lambe, Jack Holland and Christopher Ramsden, in what would once have been called a chummery. This was in 1969-70. Jack went on to postgraduate work at Essex and a career in journalism; Chris joined the British Council lecturing staff and was sent to Ethiopia. Eugene and I, me first, headed for London. Jack and Eugene are dead now, but Chris and I meet regularly since he and Amy live not far from here. It's going on fifty years since we'd walk to the end of Dun Laoghaire Pier and drink in Goggin's pub. (Irene and Clare, where are you now?) When it warmed up a bit in June I'd splash about at Sandycove — the Forty Foot — and visit Joyce's Tower in the Scotts' back garden. These were TEFLing days (my foreign students thought Ireland *triste*); TEFLing, and book-reviewing for the Dublin prints at a fiver a throw.

It was at Clifton Terrace in March, 1969, during a blue period, that I wrote 'Beyond Howth Head', first published in a limited edition a year later by the Dolmen Press. What it's about, if anything, I really don't know, though I remember the writing of it and the frame of mind I was in then: one of impatience and anomie. Impatience, I'm sorry to say, with the Ireland of those days, and an anomie of obscure personal origin. Trouble had started in the North and I was finding it hard to sort out my thoughts on the subject. Did those developments, initially cheering, presage a new, open era, or would they lead us back into the dire atavism for which the place was notorious? The answer is still unclear. I wasn't in Paris during the events of May, '68, but even in Ireland we were highly conscious of them, and they too found their way into the poem: the phrase 'exponential future', for example, was borrowed from Daniel Cohn-Bendit, 'Danny the Red', one of the student leaders. Dublin in those days contained various left-wing groups, and even Trinity had its Trotskyites, but they (we) were whistling in the dark. The Americanization of Ireland, now far advanced, was already in hand; and in any case the country at large was, and is, too set in its political ways to contemplate radical change. If the poem is about anything it's about exasperation (whence the rudery) and a growing intention, so common at that time, to take the boat train to Holyhead and Euston at the earliest opportunity — which I did in September, 1970. The London papers paid not five but £35 for a book review.

I always liked the look of Washington Square, its imposing Greek Revival houses not so much residential now as academic and functional since they belong for the most part to NYU: 'In front of them was the square, and round the corner was the more august precinct of the Fifth Avenue, taking its origin at this point with a spacious and confident air which already marked it for high destinies' (Henry James, *Washington Square*). Brian Moore describes it as it was a century later: 'I left the workroom and wandered towards Washington Square, mingling near the fountain with the phony folk singers, the adolescent Bardots . . . and the coffee-house poets clutching the latest copy of an illiterate Beat review' (*An Answer from Limbo*, 1962). Yes, but it was and is a fun place too. Memory flash, June 1991: brightly robed faculty heading in slow double file for a graduation ceremony, a grave procession through the crowd of radioheads, skateboarders and druggy types hanging out in the park. Next door to me, at 1 Fifth Ave, was NYU's Ireland House where I myself hung out much of the time when I wasn't in the Bobst Library or Bradley's jazz pub on University Place. Greenwich Village life is *village* life, and I'd often run into Sam Menashe, Joseph Brodsky or Galway Kinnell, Katha Pollitt of *The Nation* or Alice Quinn of *The New Yorker*. I had the Washington Arch under my window and 'One Fifth', an old Cunarder cocktail bar with starry ceiling, at the corner of Washington Mews, but from morning to late at night it was noisy, very noisy (traffic, rock, shenanigans), so I was relieved to move farther west, beyond 7th Ave, a short walk from the Hudson River piers. Out there, between Bleecker and West 4th, surrounded by fire escapes, I finally sat down to write my New York poem. Originally called 'The Hudson Letter', following on from 'The Yaddo Letter', it grew into more than a letter and later acquired a new title, 'New York Time': time as in time zone (EST). What's it about? About homelessness, women and global warming. There were many homeless in the city during my New York time, and I'd done some nomadism myself. Global warming was noticed, and seemed like a good thing at first. The new feminism was every-where, and dubious characters like myself had to think about pulling our socks up. I had and have many literary women friends, but a residual chauvinism prevented me from taking

American women poets, with some exceptions — Hacker, Forché — entirely seriously: there was too much special pleading, and too much vanity in play. The same could be said for us fellas of course, but women were in the ascendant and set the tone. The social tone certainly, but also the critical one, which was fine really. Didn't I start writing, at some level, in order to 'meet girls', even if I didn't know it at the time? Anyhow the idea of women, and a blithely optimistic view of global warming, presented themselves to my frozen imagination ('ten below, these nights, on average') as one and the same thing, an imaginative thaw not only personal but global. So we start with the icy river and the morning news; but what begins as a kind of letter quickly develops into something else, the description of a day as lived by a resident alien based in lower Manhattan, owing much to that famously stimulating atmosphere. I was teaching a poetry course at the time. Whitman, Crane and Elizabeth Bishop found their way into some sections; but it's an 'Anglo-Irish' piece of work, in the academic sense, or turns into one in the end. I hadn't written in verse at such length before, and had so much fun I decided to try another 'long poem' when the moment was right.

Squares, squares. Worn out by New York's climatic extremes — twenty blizzards, one a week, from November of '94 to the following spring — I returned to Dublin, to an attic flat at 45 Fitzwilliam Square: an informal arrangement, there was no lease. The landlord Eoghan Ganly, a genial fellow, acted for his aged mother Bridget, an artist whose youthful self-portrait hung in the entrance hall. Other tenants included Muriel, a librarian, and Helen, a young journalist; the psychiatrist Anthony Clare had consulting rooms on the ground floor. When his mother died Eoghan decided to sell the house and gave us all six months' notice; so off I went to Kinsale again as I'd long wanted to do — and not without relief. No. 45, with a key to the garden (crocuses there too, also lilac and laburnum), was a great spot but had serious drawbacks: limited space, and the tourist 'coaches' that drew up every five minutes to photograph the decorative door next door. 'A typical Dublin dower', the tour guides would announce, though it was not. (I never saw her use it, but Helen had a pump-action water gun for tour groups that got too close.) Mysterious steps could often be heard on the roof; blackbirds, confused by blazing arc lights, sang in the dead of night. Despite the central location and cultural history I found myself in the invidious position of starting to dislike Georgian architecture, the high townhouse variety at least: its monotonous, intimidating aspect; the fetishism. The big brass knob on the front door was nicked in the wee hours — clink, clink: what . . . ? — and exposed intercom wires ripped out: those houses, and what they represented, displeased nihilistic youths from the discos in Leeson St., as once they displeased Swift when the first façades appeared on the north side of the city. (He saw it as a property scam.) But the combination of cultural history and contemporary chaos, together with the imminent millennium, had me thinking along *fin-de-siècle* lines. When the swish of homegoing traffic died down each evening I'd set myself to re-reading relevant texts: Symons, Huysmans, Wilde. 'The Yellow Book' was a provisional title, and too specific, so it too acquired a new one: 'Decadence'.

A city thing, decadence, and I was tired of cities. Advancing years demanded a slower pace and a new compact with 'nature', albeit domesticated nature. The environmental writer Roderic Knowles, a frequent visitor here, describes an epiphany in a Kerry wood: 'the trees, all oaks, were no longer simply trunks, branches, twigs and leaves . . . A tree, like other living things, is indivisibly both energy and matter. It is first and foremost a *field of energy*, its material aspect being an outer, denser expression of this.' Scots pine, larch, alder, oak and the rest protect us from high winds at the Grove; woodpigeons, grumbling softly among themselves, roost in beeches. And here's the sea, or at least the inner harbour with its tinkling yacht basin. Still interested in the long(ish) discursive poem, I sat at my window desk and came up with 'Harbour Lights' and 'Dreams of a Summer Night' — the first title borrowed from Jimmy Kennedy, the second suggested by Ingmar Bergman's *Smiles of a Summer Night* and a favourite Shakespeare play. They came with surprising ease since the Grove, in Knowles's phrase, is a field of energy, and an inspiration. The place itself wrote 'Dreams', and in saying this I can shift responsibility, and criticism, on to 'nature' and sustain the not-so-lonely impulse of delight I knew in younger years when I played goofy golf and silly billiards against myself so I couldn't lose. Oh, optimal conditions!

The Swimmer as Hero

A wild splasher, though not much of a 'wild' swimmer as such, I was awed and humbled by Charles Sprawson's reports of his achievements when I first read *Haunts of the Black Masseur* (1992), his inspired history of natation, in America *The Swimmer as Hero*. I'd known him slightly in earlier days and remembered him as a tall, muscular figure, quietly enigmatic. I wasn't to know then that in his own mind he really lived under water much of the time — deep water, the 'black masseur' whose strong hands grapple and galvanize the serious aquaphile. (There used also to be a famous *real* black masseur at the New Orleans Athletic Club, of whom more in a minute.) Growing up in India, where his father was a headmaster, Sprawson learned to swim in a palace pool 'among columns that disappeared mysteriously into black water', and plunged happily into the Indian Ocean. 'Though very young, I began to form a vague conception of the swimmer as someone rather remote and divorced from everyday life . . . It seemed to me that [swimming] appealed to the introverted and eccentric, individualists involved in a mental world of their own.' A classicist, one who knows his way around Greece and Rome, he writes of the feeling for water that runs through Roman life and poetry, 'their sense of its charm and divinity that they derived from the Greeks' whose spring waters were often consecrated as shrines to local deities. Oracles established themselves in their vicinities: 'Greek civilization seemed to revolve around water.' Archaeology, however, has unearthed 'only a few trickles on the sites of ancient springs'. Sprawson finds these trickles on his travels. The Clitumnus and Bandusian springs have been fenced off besides, though fences don't deter this resourceful author. Resourceful and erudite: 'The great central hall of Diocletian's Baths was converted by

Michelangelo into a church, and the superb granite columns, each hewn out of a single block forty feet in height, still remain as they were in the imperial heyday.' The excavation of Pompeian pools, decorated with tritons and naiads, revealed the intensity of the Roman love of bathing: 'They were accustomed to say of an ignorant man, "He neither knows how to read or swim."' But with the fall of Rome water came to be seen as a bad thing, detrimental to health, 'a breeding ground for rats, a source of plague and disease'; and the Church took a dim view. Swimming became unfashionable, even wicked, and re-mained so until the Romantic era. There are some faintly homoerotic moments in Sprawson's text, but don't be deceived.

Leander's nightly swims to Sestos from Abydos intrigued several poets, to speak only of poets, including Marlowe and Coleridge. (Marlowe implies the intrepid lover used the breast-stroke; his arms 'opened wide at every stroke'.) It was Byron who first performed the feat for the 19th century. Although a fan, Poe pooh-poohed the achievement. The current is strong and swift, but the strait there little more than a mile wide. Poe himself claimed to have swum, as a boy, six miles up the James River in Virginia against the tide; but Byron retains the romantic-hero championship. Water, though, filled Poe's imagination, appearing frequently, and seldom benignly, in the stories ('A Descent into the Maelstrom') and poems:

> *Resignedly beneath the sky*
> *The melancholy waters lie.*
> *No rays from the holy heaven come down*
> *On the long night-time of that town.*
> ('The City in the Sea')

Sprawson, accompanied by his daughter, did the Hellespont swim himself (they swam sidestroke to avoid looking down). He makes the useful point that Byron wasn't interested in what lay beneath the surface: 'There are no descriptions in his work of underwater scenes.' He wasn't a contemplative swimmer but a competitive one. He liked to move fast and win: 'It suggests the superficiality of his imagination, and his nerve, that he should

be one of the first to swim over dark waters and great depths
. . . His genius was for the surface of life.' Many poets —
Whitman and Swinburne, Valéry, Brooke and Crane — were
keen on the stuff. 'A first-rate aquatic loafer,' said Whitman, 'I
possessed almost unlimited capacity for floating on my back';
but he dreamed of more than this. Only a bather himself, he
admired strong swimmers and celebrated them in 'Sleep-
Chasings' and 'I Sing the Body Electric'. A constant shore-
walker, as recorded in *Specimen Days* and 'Elemental Drifts'
('As I ebbed with the ocean of life . . . '), he kept his eye on the
bigger picture. Whitman's admirer and 'fellow seabird'
Swinburne, who shared his 'amorous' relations with the waves,
liked nothing better than a good thrashing by high wintry seas.
Paul Valéry, who as a youth swam daily below the Cimetière
Marin at Sète, spoke of his frequent *'fornication avec l'onde'*.
Rupert Brooke swam in the rivers around Cambridge, else-
where in England, and in the South Seas — Hawaii, Tahiti —
where he found 'the senses and perceptions more lordly and
acute'. In his Grantchester days, says Sprawson, Brooke would
often swim in the river at night by the light of a bicycle lamp:
'It was here that he swam naked with Virginia Woolf, in the
dark water "smelling of mint and mud".' (Iris Murdoch, later,
was also a keen freshwater swimmer.) Brooke welcomed the
opening of hostilities in 1914, likening the many young recruits
to 'swimmers into cleanness leaping', but didn't live to see the
ensuing cataclysm, dying at sea on his way to Gallipoli — 'a
swimmer's war', says Sprawson, which 'brought to a bitter
conclusion the English infatuation with Leander'. Hart Crane
took his last dive from the stern of the *Orizaba*.

Diving for most, says Sprawson, was 'merely a means of entering
the water, until the Swedes swept the board at the 1900 Paris
Olympics'; then the Germans took over. The Weimar years were
notable for many things: art, music, theatre, cinema and sport,
including swimming and diving. Defeat in the first world war,
and subsequent humiliation, seem to have stimulated a defiant
national spirit both beneficial and problematic. Against a back-
ground of intense political conflict a cult of 'pathic health'

(Adorno's phrase) arose; though this wasn't unprecedented. Sprawson takes us back to Goethe, who liked to swim in freezing water. Thousands followed his example; for him a cold bathe 'transformed bourgeois sensual exhaustion into a fresh and vigorous existence'. Swimming metaphors crowded into his work. Besides the amniotic fun and games, this was an almost political gesture. Not revolutionary exactly (he swam with titled folk) but bracing, inspirational. Sprawson revisits Leni Riefenstahl's creative 'documentary' *Olympische Spiele* (1936), concentrating on the climactic high-diving sequence, where the divers seem released from all earthly restrictions, even gravity, like 'mythical figures . . . against a cloudy, ominous sky'. The Americans, says Sprawson, were the stars of the diving scenes, and they had been the world's fastest swimmers for many years. Swimming, from Hiawatha and Mark Twain to the present, has had an important place in American culture. Whitman, as we've seen, was keen. Jack London, aged eighteen, deliberately let himself drift out to sea off San Francisco and nearly drowned: 'a drunken attempt at suicide' but also 'a delirious experience', says Sprawson. He too, like Brooke, swam in Hawaii, and his article 'A Royal Sport' helped to revive the declining art of surfing among the Hawaiians. A surface swimmer like Byron, he was fascinated by waves and would analyze their various qualities: the 'amazing peacock blue', the 'smoking' breakers of California beaches where he and his athletic wife Charmian would swim out dangerously far as a matter of course. He fictionalized their married life and 'devotes several pages to the resentment felt by the emasculated tourists towards this dazzling pair, as if they were heroic anachronisms, relics of saga and romance and out of place'. London saw their lives in mythical terms, as Scott and Zelda Fitzgerald were later to do. Sprawson is well up on pool-crazy William Randolph Hearst's opulent 'Roman' baths at San Simeon, and on Tennessee Williams, whose Sebastian Venable in *Suddenly Last Summer* 'couldn't stay out of the water'. Neither could his creator. Beaches and pools, says Sprawson, were for Williams places of seduction where 'he could entice young men with his charm and didn't have to rely, like Sebastian, on a sister extended as bait in a transparent costume'. Sprawson made a point of swimming at the New Orleans Athletic Club on North Rampart St. — 'after which it seemed only proper to submit myself to the hands of the black masseur who mangled the poor clerk in the Williams story ['Desire and the Black Masseur'] and still haunts the premises' — or did at the time of writing.

Another Williams, Esther, who won championships before the war, joined Rose's Aquacades and starred in the film *Neptune's Daughter* (1949). She was, says Sprawson, 'the last and most successful of the many beautiful swimming stars tempted by Hollywood, who could dive as elegantly as they swam'. A private pool had become *the* status symbol: 'Their tropical profusion charmed Hockney as his plane flew low over the city before he landed in Los Angeles for the first time.' Hockney's pool pictures represent the culmination of Hollywood's fascination with captive water. Pools became important accessories not just socially but in films themselves. Think of the pool that begins and ends *Sunset Boulevard* (1950), where the William Holden character, who 'always wanted a pool', finishes up dead in one — as did Jay Gatsby of course. There's evidently some psychic connection between captive water and death, some bitter thing, *amarum aliquid*, in the faux paradise of the American Dream. 'A pool is misapprehended,' says Joan Didion in her essay 'Holy Water' (*The White Album*, 1979), 'as a trapping of affluence, real or pretended, and of hedonistic attention to the body. Actually a pool is . . . a symbol not of affluence but of order, of control over the uncontrollable.' The history of LA water is not a pretty one. It's transported, says Sprawson, 'hundreds of miles . . . from the Owens Valley and the Colorado River, after the gradual and sinister process of acquisition recorded in Polanski's film *Chinatown*.' There water runs not downhill but 'towards money'.

The late Roger Deakin, a founder member of Friends of the Earth, casts a cold eye on the de-wilding and commodification of water in *Waterlog* (1999): 'More and more places and things are signposted, labelled and officially "interpreted". There is something about all this that is turning the reality of things into virtual reality. It's the reason why walking, cycling and swimming will always be subversive activities.' The safety industry plays its part in this, whence also the disappearance of springboards. A dive was once a gesture of respect, a genuflection to water; now we just jump, feet first, as if contemptuously. John Cheever's story 'The Swimmer', and the Burt Lancaster film of the same title, to which Sprawson refers, have come to be a sort of foundation myth for swimming writers. Ned Merrill, no longer young, sets out one Sunday afternoon to swim home from a Long Island party via his neighbours' pools. He feels himself to be a heroic figure, superior to the series of poolside neighbours with their money talk and hangovers; then things start to go wrong: 'He had swum too long, been immersed too long.' Deakin, who acknowledges Sprawson's 'modern swimming classic', acknowledges Cheever too. *Waterlog* is the diary of a Britain-wide series of swims from pool to sea to pool, from the Scillies to the Hebrides, from Wales to the Wash, and home to a moated house in Suffolk, where Deakin would also swim. He too, like Sprawson, describes the egotistical sublime of the swimming life: 'Once in the water, you are immersed in an intensely private world as you were in the womb.' He notes the close relationship between swimming and music (rhythm), and not only the delight but the dangers to mind and body: 'Skirting the edge of the sea and daydreaming like this, I was also skirting the boundaries of unconsciousness, the line between dreaming and drowning.' Not drowning but waving, I once swam the Bandon River at Kilmacsimon where it's still tidal, meeting with waterweed and a strong current, and felt the same. A native of Champagne, the great Gaston Bachelard was thirty before he saw the sea, which he found a bit 'banal', and in *L'Eau et les rêves* (*Water and Dreams*, 1999) praises the oneiric qualities of streams and lakes: '*l'eau douce est la véritable eau mythique*' ('fresh water is the true mythic water'). True, but the fate of streams and rivers is to become sea, the greatest earthly myth, the largest tangible thing (three quarters of the globe) and our best personal experience of the infinite.

The Rain Bridge: A Story for Rory

There once was a boy who fell in love with a bridge. It was a beautiful bridge, made of fine old wood, with spaces between the timbers and railings along each side. It crossed a stream that ran down from the hills and out to sea, with woods to left and right. The boy walked across it every day. Not just once, or twice, or even three times; but backwards and forwards, backwards and forwards, the boy would cross the bridge he loved. Sometimes he sat and stroked the wood. Sometimes he lay down flat and gazed into the water. It was the most beautiful bridge in the whole world! 'I love you, bridge,' he said.

One day it started to rain. The rain grew heavier. It rained and rained, for days and days. The boy stayed at home and waited for it to stop. He sat at the window drawing a picture of raindrops running down the glass, and wondered about the bridge. He felt sorry for it, cold and wet out there in the wind and rain, his beautiful bridge. Meanwhile the heavy rain fell on the hills, and the stream became a river, and the river became a torrent, and the bridge the boy loved was washed away.

Next morning the rain stopped, the sun shone, and there were rainbows. Steam rose from the roofs of the houses, and the roads, and the woods, as if it was the first day of the world. The boy woke up, looked out of the window, and saw that the rain had stopped. Excited, he washed his face, pulled on his clothes and rushed out of the house. He ran along the road, and through the woods, to see the bridge he loved . . . But the bridge had disappeared! He looked down the river, and out to sea, but there was no sign of the bridge; only a rainbow bridged the two sides of the stream. So he sat down on the ground and began to cry. He cried and cried, and stared at the brimming stream, while tears ran down his face like raindrops down a window. He knew that the bridge he loved was gone for ever.

While he sat there, sniffing and wiping his eyes, a big man came along. The big man looked at where the bridge had been, and looked at the boy. 'What's wrong, lad?' said the man. 'Are you crying about the bridge?' He had a kind face. The boy nodded and dried his eyes. 'It was a fine bridge,' said the man, 'but the river must have flooded and washed it away.' Together they looked in silence at where the bridge had been. 'I know,' said the man. 'We'll make a new bridge. It won't be as good as the old one, of course, but at least it will be a bridge. What do you think?'

The boy was still sad, but he nodded at the man; and so they set to work. For a week, while the sun shone and the river changed back to a stream, the man brought planks, and a hammer and nails. The boy held the nails and watched while the big man built the bridge. At last it was finished and they walked across it together, backwards and forwards, backwards and forwards. It was a lovely bridge. Not as nice as the old one, of course, but very nice even so.

That day the big man had to leave. He walked across the bridge for the last time, waved goodbye, and vanished into the woods. Now the boy was left alone on the bridge, and he felt shy. He sat down very slowly and stroked the wood. After a while he lay down flat and gazed into the water. He lay there a long time until it began to get dark, and he thought, 'It's not the bridge I loved, of course, nothing can ever replace *that*; but it *is* a beautiful bridge.' And he walked home.

That night, as he lay in bed, he thought of moonlight shining down on the bridge — and, strangely enough, he couldn't be sure if it was the old bridge or the *new* bridge that he saw; for they both looked much the same. He knew that the old bridge was the one he really loved; but he didn't cry any more. He knew too that he would go to the new bridge every day and stroke the wood, and gaze into the water, and be happy. He fell asleep and dreamed of bridges, and hills, and rain, and sun, and rivers, and of the sea where all the rivers go, and dreamed that one day he, too, would be a big man and able to build bridges.

While he slept the moon shone down on the new bridge where he would go next day, and the day after, and the day after that, and on all the bridges everywhere that he had yet to cross; for the world is full of bridges, some old, some new, some big, some small — so many you couldn't count them.

~

There now, that's the story. 'It's awful sad,' said Rory Mahon, six years old, when I wrote it down and read it to him; and so it is in a way, though it picks up at the end. Done at a time of marital indecision, this 35-year-old yarn sounds, looks, in retrospect, oddly autobiographical. I'm the 'big man' I suppose (I wish), forty or so at the time, though I couldn't fix a bridge to save my life. We're talking here, I think, about a tributary of the River Bush, at or near Bushmills, Co. Antrim, where they make the whiskey. An old bridge was in fact split apart that summer by troubled waters. Doreen and I, too, were split apart by troubled waters, and never really got it together again. There was to be no lasting renewal of the bridge for us, though each of us found new bridges to cross since the world is full of bridges, 'some old, some new, some big, some small — so many you couldn't count them'.

My personal choice would include the bridge at Cushendun in the Antrim Glens some miles from Bushmills, Shaw's Bridge over the Lagan in Belfast, Dublin's Ha'penny Bridge, the Hungerford, Brooklyn and Golden Gate bridges. The Hungerford Bridge? Yes, the railway and pedestrian bridge from London's Charing X to the South Bank. (I was taken, long ago, to visit the artist Topolski in an enclosed arch where he had his amazing studio.) The Golden Gate because of the San Francisco song and a drive, once, with the poet Sara Berkeley, my ex-student. The Brooklyn Bridge because of that very Rory, now forty himself, for whom the bridge story was written. Retrieving an old copy after years of neglect I thought again about publishing it as a children's book and asked the artist Sarah Iremonger to think about illustrations. We researched bridges real and imaginary: footbridges, road bridges, suspension and cantilever bridges, viaducts, bridges in the sky, cloud bridges.

My first significant bridge was the one at Cushendun ('foot of the river Dun'). A short, four-arched 19th-century road bridge, it could take only one vehicle at a time in the 1950s but has long since been widened. I used to go there with a school friend, a not-too-distant neighbour who lived on the Cavehill Road, and spend, by special arrangement (family friends), Whitsun weekends and the last two weeks of August at MacBride's Hotel with its old-fashioned ambience and its Blue Room bar, a traditional-music venue. We were too young — fourteen, fifteen — to take an interest in the Blue Room, but we filled the daylight hours with swimming, 'rounders' behind the beach and hanging out with contemporaries, some local, some of them visitors like ourselves. Evenings might find us playing board games with the artist Maurice Wilks and family at their holiday 'caravan' in a field by the soft light of an oil lamp; but the bridge was our social centre. Bigger bridges were waiting. Rory, who loved the old bridge that the rain swept away ('Daddy, I love this bridge'), later fell in love with the Brooklyn Bridge, that great pedestrian rainbow over New York's East River once celebrated by Hart Crane. One of the magical first suspension bridges ('How could mere toil align thy choiring strings?'), it joins the romantic bridges of old Europe with its poetic presence. It too, like the Bushmills one, is a boardwalk footbridge, though very *much* bigger of course, with traffic streaming past on either side. Another boardwalk footbridge, this one in Paris, the Pont des Arts, from the Quai de Conti to the Quai du Louvre, became a favourite when, some years ago, I spent time at the Hôtel La Louisiane — in circular room 19 as it used to be, with its upside-down, street-in-the-ceiling acoustics. Looking down the rue de Seine I couldn't see the bridge from my desk window, academic buildings intervened; but I knew it was there, reminding me of Bushmills and the bridge a little boy loved.

Readings

Poetry has been sung, and read aloud, since ancient times; but the present craze is little more than fifty years old. Readings were previously rare, special events of an 'elitist' character, until the dramatic examples of Dylan Thomas and Allen Ginsberg made them popular; and soon, in the 1960s, they became an established and widespread phenomenon, like rock concerts. Huge crowds turned out to listen to Yevtushenko, and in America to the Beats. The Poetry International series filled London's South Bank Centre for a week every summer (I remember Neruda and Lowell). Universities, and local societies backed by Arts Council funds, introduced regular reading programmes; festivals sprang up. All this delighted 'poetry lovers' everywhere. It's proved a useful source of income for poets themselves, sold books and provided paid-for travel at home and abroad — in my own case, for example, to France (often), to Russia, India and various American destinations: the Ivy League 'schools', the Midwest, the South and California including Berkeley. But I don't do it any more. I tired of readings, and of travel; so, although it might have been nice to visit Japan, for instance, I declined. This retirement from performance, even in Britain and Ireland, was gradual, selective and due in part to the nature of the exercise itself. It was fun for a long time, much of the time; but, like other performing poets, I suspect, I found the meretricious aspect increasingly wearisome. Self-disgust wasn't far off. I've been present at fine readings, it must be said: Ted Hughes at the Institute of Contemporary Arts, London; Geoffrey Hill in a Westminster church; Nuala Ní Dhomhnaill at NYU. Hughes read *Crow* (1970), a hair-raising experience. Hill, scary in black with red socks, read his great Péguy poem slowly and forcefully. Nuala read a dual-language selection from *Pharaoh's Daughter* (1990). Also in New

York, at the 92nd St. 'Y', a Dante night with translations from the *Inferno* by various hands. Readings, especially of striking new work, can be as exciting and enriching as the best theatre, with which they have so much in common — though actors, with some exceptions (thank you Stephen Rea), tend to poeticize and elocutionize, with excruciating results. Better the rough Yorkshire residue in Hughes's voice, the uncompromising severity in Hill's, or Nuala's gay, almost throwaway presentation: the personal delivery, as heard in the head at the moment of composition. Grigson laid down that poems must only be read on the page, also that good poets 'mumble' and are hard to hear; but this is an English class thing. What about Yeats with his declamatory brogue (his recorded voice survives)? Even Tennyson rumbled rather than mumbled: you can listen to him rumbling 'The Charge of the Light Brigade', one of the first captured on wax cylinders and later re-recorded.

We used to play an old Caedmon 78 of Eliot, Stevens, Graves and the 'Thirties' poets. Graves mumbled a bit all right, and Auden too, in their clipped, deprecating Oxford manner. Eliot's voice, like his features, had a 'clerical cut'; Stevens bodied forth his idea of order in the sort of East Coast accent you might have heard from an old-time Harvard graduate. But these were of the past. The poetic voice has been democratized, or re-democratized. Burns, after all, spoke lowland Scots; Keats, they say, spoke Cockney; and even Coleridge retained traces of Somerset. Now regional sounds are heard again, and have been for many years: Ulster, Clydeside, Tyneside, Mersey. Dylan Thomas never abandoned his sonorous Welsh intonation, nor Heaney his soft South Derry one; the Liverpool poets remained recognizably Liverpudlian. But poets, so often outsiders in their communities of origin, may find themselves speaking in more deliberate tones, the detached interior voice that dictates the poems. Education has much to do with this, but even formal education only develops a singularity which was already there. Be that as it may, an unmediated voice, like a physical presence, can — *pace* Grigson — add to the page by acquainting us personally with the poet for better or worse; often for worse. Poetry, a human activity, can benefit from the human contact, audience and reader both. I listened to Christopher Reid's selection from *A Scattering* (2009), poems to and about his late wife, was greatly moved, and read the book page by page (did she have radiotherapy?):

> *a glimpse of her own*
> *undimmable spirit:*
> *'I'm being radiant*
> *again, aren't I!'*
> *It was inspired,*
> *brave, funny and subtle.*

Hearing it read aloud you're in touch with the person who wrote it, and with the absent person who inspired it; and this can only vitalize and deepen the experience. I sensed too that Chris was getting something back from us, the audience: his reading of these poems, I thought, is a *requiescat*, his 'sharing' or 'working through' (forgive the jargon) an inclusive act of commemoration, like a memorial service. I'm being impertinent here perhaps; but a similar sort of thing could be said of any sincere articulation of that kind. Sadly too many readings, including my own at times, have been little more than a showing-off, and in need of a different kind of propitiation — or expiation. But poetry began as narration and song. A ghost of song, or at least of incantation, has to be evident, so the heard voice is a natural feature of the poetic enterprise; and only the author can do it right, even if he or she mumbles, which may be the right way to do it for some authors. Stage presence and virtuosity can be distracting. We aren't rock stars; we have to behave ourselves.

More demanding than the mumble, for poet and audience both, is the chronic stammer. John Montague stammered repeatedly, a result of early traumas — which didn't prevent him being mischievous, or doing readings. He persisted, and usually overcame the problem. The stammer was a recurrent theme, even a function of the work, seeming to dictate its hesitant rhythms and linebreaks. A childhood relocation from Brooklyn to Tyrone affected him deeply for good and ill: for ill in the separation from his parents; for good in that he was returned to a once bilingual community whose heritage he would celebrate in his long poem *The Rough Field*:

> *The last Gaelic speaker in the parish*
> *When I stammered my school Irish*
> *One Sunday after Mass, crinkled*
> *A rusty litany of praise:*
> Tá an Ghaeilge againn arís . . . *

Poets live in their poems; biographies often miss the point. We offer ourselves as illustrative data, even as historical symptoms, even as scapegoats. Poets in person explain a lot. An audience will register tone and nuance, and better understand the puzzling bits; above all it will glimpse the organic source of the work. It may not like what it sees or hears; but then the reader may not either, in which case we have a failure on our hands and we've all wasted an evening.

Worst is the reader who goes on too long. The event should last for an hour at most, including intro and question time if any: no one can take in more. Best is the 'rap' or group reading, which might run to an hour and a half, ten or fifteen minutes each. Worst for the reader is the long queue of autograph hunters: a personal grouch, but one must be gracious. (A short queue, or none at all, when others are busily signing, is equally bothersome.) Why this tedious chore when you want to relax with friends you haven't seen for a while? An extension of the organic principle, I expect: a trace of the joined-up writing. At least they don't tear the clothes off you, though that might be fun in other circumstances. I think it was the American theologian Paul Tillich who was asked by his wife, after fifty happy years, why he continued giving lectures at distant venues. 'On the off-chance I'll meet,' said he, 'the woman in my life.' Naughty.

*We have the Irish again.

Ragtime

'The little boy stood at the end of the porch and fixed his gaze on a bluebottle fly traversing the screen in a way that made it appear to be coming up the hill from North Avenue. The fly flew off. An automobile was coming up the hill from North Avenue. As it drew closer he saw it was a black 45-horsepower Pope-Toledo Runabout.' This photogenic moment early in the late E. L. ('Ed') Doctorow's novel *Ragtime* (1975) anticipates several things: the film camera, the triumph of the motor car, the informative precision (or plausibility) of the story about to unfold, and the cinematic nature of the 'American' century. It's 1906 in the prosperous New York suburb of New Rochelle where the little boy's family lives. Father is in the business of manufacturing patriotic decorations and fireworks, Mother is a seemingly placid housewife; both are pillars of local Wasp society. Mother's younger brother, who lives with them, is a difficult young man having trouble 'finding himself'. Grandfather, once a teacher, tells the little boy stories from Ovid which 'proposed to him that the forms of life were volatile and that everything in the world could as easily be something else' — a theme the novel itself develops. Against a newsy period background in heightened resolution, a mixture of fiction and fact (Harry Houdini, J. P. Morgan, Emma Goldman), we follow the fortunes of two unnamed families, the New Rochelle one and an immigrant Jewish one on the Lower East Side of Manhattan consisting of Tateh, Mameh and their little girl. Harry K. Thaw, heir to a coal fortune and abusive husband of famous beauty Evelyn Nesbit, is on trial (fact) for the murder of architect Stanford White, her previous protector, and the anarchist Goldman (fact) is stirring things up all over the place when Father, an amateur explorer, goes off (fiction) with Peary's third expedition to the Arctic. He returns nine months later to find things at home rather different. Mother and her younger brother have been running the business in his absence; his patriarchal authority is diminished. Bridget, the housemaid, has also moved with the times: (she) 'put a record on the Victrola, wound the crank and sat in the parlor smoking a cigarette and listening to John McCormack sing "I Hear You Calling Me" . . . She was no longer efficient or respectful.' Even more to the point, a silent young black woman, Sarah, is now in residence upstairs with her baby, born out of wedlock. The father, a black guy and Harlem jazz musician, comes calling, and in due course persuades shy Sarah to marry him. His speciality is the ragtime music of Scott Joplin, which he demonstrates on the family's out-of-tune piano. (Doctorow's people had a music shop in the Bronx.)

Kleist, author of *Prince Friedrich of Homburg* and other plays, also wrote short fiction, later much admired by Kafka for example. Among the longest and best-known stories are 'The Marquise of O— ' and 'Michael Kohlhaas' (1810), based on 'an old chronicle'. Kohlhaas, a 16th-century Brandenburg horse dealer, sets out to sell some horses at Dresden in neighbouring Saxony. At the border he's told he now needs a special permit; but this is a gratuitous and insulting imposition made up by a nasty local landowner, the Junker von Tronka. Leaving a pair of yearlings as surety, Kohlhaas proceeds to Dresden. Stopping at Tronka Castle on his way home, he finds the yearlings in terrible condition, having been ill-used by the Junker and his men. Taking the influential Tronka to law, he gets no satisfaction; a petition to the ruling Elector of Saxony falls on deaf ears. To make a long story short, Kohlhaas and his friends resort to violence, burning down Tronka Castle and part of Wittenberg, where the Junker is thought to be hiding. Soon the whole countryside is up in arms; Kohlhaas's wife is killed. Despite Martin Luther's personal intervention Kohlhaas, though a God-fearing man, persists in his private war, finally obtaining justice of a sort at the cost of his own life; and the tale ends. Doctorow adopts this framework for his main narrative. Sarah's piano-playing fiancé is one Coalhouse Walker Jr., of

Manhattan's Clef Club Orchestra, a courteous but determined man, smartly turned out, the proud owner of a shining new Model T Ford. Driving away one day from the house in New Rochelle, he finds the road blocked by men of the Emerald Isle fire station, who demand a toll: 'We need the money for a firetruck, the Chief explained. So we can drive to fires just like you drive to whorehouses.' Coalhouse refuses, and walks off into town to check with the police. Returning to the car he finds it vandalized and befouled. The cops are no help. Coalhouse leaves the scene, determined on legal action; but lawyers are no help either. Sarah dies in an attempt to intervene. Coalhouse now goes underground with a group of followers, young blacks like himself. The fire station is blown up and destroyed, the first of several; men are killed. A reign of terror ensues. Coalhouse demands the restoration of his car to its original condition, and the delivery of fire chief Willie Conklin, the worst offender, to his personal justice; but Conklin has taken refuge in the Bronx. The action escalates. The Coalhouse group occupies the famous Morgan Library on 36th St., wire it for dynamite and reiterate their demands. The authorities get the great black educator Booker T. Washington to intercede. He and Coalhouse confer under a Cranach portrait of Luther in the West Room, but Coalhouse is adamant; and I'll leave him there in case you haven't read the book.

Mameh and Tateh separate. Tateh takes the little girl (how does she feel about this?) and, leaving the Lower East Side, they go on their travels, winding up in Philadelphia. Artistic skills (he is a street artist by trade) draw him into the embryonic movie business, where at last he begins to thrive and 'point his life along the lines of flow of American energy'. Mother and Father have separated too. He goes down with the *Lusitania* while taking to England some of his own explosive materials which 'undoubtedly contributed to the monstrous detonations that preceded its abrupt sinking'. Mother, on holiday with the kids in Atlantic City, takes up with Tateh and his little girl: for them, at least, there's a happy ending. There are other surprises, some relating to Mother's younger brother; but, besides the story, *Ragtime* is about other things too, notably recurrent patterns in history, of which we're given many hints and, in the Morgan chapters, some scholarly exposition. (J. P., having ransacked Europe for his Library, has now gone further back and is working on ancient Egypt.) A tankard containing a note from Coalhouse is thrown from a Library window: 'The object, now dented, was a medieval drinking stein of silver with a hunting scene in relief. The curator asked to see it and advised that it was from the seventeenth century and had belonged to the Elector of Saxony' — an allusion to Kleist's story. You might say that Doctorow transforms legend (Kleist) into something resembling a modern myth. What with Coalhouse (Kohlhaas) and Booker T. (Luther), there's a lot of metempsychosis going on. Even Henry Ford is said to resemble one of the Pharaohs. Morgan invites him to lunch and explains his theory of 'a beneficent magic available to certain men of every age for the use of mankind'; known as the *prisca theologia*, this belief system (derived from Giordano Bruno, the Rosicrucians and ultimately from Hermes Trismegistus, Morgan says) supposedly survives from century to century, and the 'transcendentally gifted' are with us even now: 'They come back, you see? They come back!' And here's a pair of them in a brownstone mansion on 36th St., Morgan himself and the improbable Ford. These are the ones who make the world go round. Together they found 'the most secret and exclusive club in America, the Pyramid, of which they were the only members. It endowed certain researches which persist to this day.' In pursuit of his own researches, Morgan visits Egypt and spends a night in the Great Pyramid at Giza, staring into the dark and waiting for 'whatever signs Osiris might deign to bring him'; but he is shown no signs. Not, at least, until he emerges in the morning to find a sign of the times: the New York Giants in baseball suits perched all over the Great Sphinx, having their photographs taken in the course of a world exhibition tour. Morgan, who has caught a chill, goes into a decline and doesn't recover. But he's decided his illness is a sign from Osiris, and dies happy. All this is highly entertaining; but, whatever Doctorow's own beliefs, the book relies for its lasting impact on the depth of field provided by the documentary material and historical echoes. *Ragtime* was first published in the era of Martin Luther King and various Black Power groupings, when many whites feared the spectre of civic unrest and even the threat of revolutionary race war such as often seem, in the States, not far from the surface. Doctorow's own radical interests (see also *The Book of Daniel*, 1971) inspired not only the narrative itself but the graphic trenchancy of its presentation. Not so much a novel, perhaps, as a slide show of American life at the time, this once bestselling work deserves a revival — especially now when symptoms of unrestrained capitalism are once again in lurid flower; not that they ever went away.

Caravans

What do we call them, caravans or trailers? Once denoting a camel train of traders in the desert somewhere between, say, Baghdad and Tehran, and resting at caravanserais (road houses), the word 'caravan' was adopted in the early 20th century to mean car-a-van (in America 'trailer' as in 'trailer trash'). Trailer makes more sense but means something different, depending where you are; so let's stick with 'caravan', the house on wheels with a tow hitch. George Borrow, author of *Lavengro* and *The Romany Rye*, lived for some years at Great Yarmouth, Norfolk — where once, for two summer months, I had my own trailer-trash moment. This was in student days when many would spend July canning fruit or peas in East Anglia to finance August travels on the Continent. In this instance there were half a dozen of us from Dublin and Belfast working the bar of a seaside caravan camp. Our living conditions were primitive: 'What a bunch of tinkers', I heard someone remark. I again kipped in a caravan some years later while staying with a hippy commune on an old farm near Grimaud (Var), so I've been a Provençal 'tinker' too — though this rough interlude was followed, I admit, by a restorative couple of nights at a *Relais Routier* in St.-Tropez. At one time horse-drawn vans of the colourful kind could be hired for self-catering holidays. You'd see them in Wicklow, Kerry and Connemara, though the idea never really caught on: too much like work, I expect, and motorists didn't like them. But the car-a-van survives, and even semi-retired ones have second lives as holiday homes. Derelict and fully retired, they rot on patches of earth and scrub in crowded yards, overgrown gardens and barren precarious corners of cliff-top fields. Eyesores, say some; but no, each has its own romance. The rickety chimney suggests a diminutive stove within, bunk beds, an antique radio, limited washing facilities, the bucket of water from a spring or a standing pipe; but the door is probably locked and the key lost.

Covered wagons were ubiquitous in Wild West books and films, but modern caravan lit. is surprisingly scarce. *The Grapes of Wrath*? Not quite. Steinbeck's Joad family head west in an old Hudson Sedan with the top back-half removed to form a truck for their belongings — though Al later reports that 'a fella's buildin' a house trailer. Right over there. Back a them tents. Got beds an' a stove — ever'thing. Jus' live in her.' There's one in Brian Moore's *The Mangan Inheritance* (1979), set in West Cork: 'The splendid panorama was marred by a yellow caravan trailer [still there], up on wooden blocks in a field on the right. From the trailer on a clothesline . . . sheets and miscellaneous garments flapped like the flags of poverty. A quiff of smoke rose toward the sky from a dirty exhaust vent. Someone was at home . . . ' Marina Lewycka's *Two Caravans* (2007), *Strawberry Fields* in the US, about migrant fruit pickers in Kent, is to be recommended; and cheeky chappie Richard Hammond, formerly of the BBC's *Top Gear* motoring programme, has published *A Short History of Caravans in the UK* (2009), an illustrated and not very funny send-up of the subject. There are, of course, periodicals for enthusiasts and trashy paperbacks for the depraved, with bad girls posing provocatively on trailer steps, but these are a far cry from the traditional picture. 'In Ireland, which has more than its share of vagrants in the form of gypsies and tinkers and where the migratory instinct has been a fact of history,' wrote Stephens and Greene in their life of Synge, 'the vagrant and the ordinary tramp are never looked upon as outcasts or degenerates. For Synge — indeed for many writers and painters — the vagrant is the personification of a romantic element in life and an antidote to the devouring concern for land.' Synge thought in terms of tramps, not vans, but the same thing applies. The romantic element is fainter now as regards 'tinkers', to say the least, the devouring concern for property greater than ever; but the migratory instinct, though submerged, survives. This is by no means unique to Ireland: think of France, Spain, Romania. In fact, with whole populations seemingly on

the move, in Africa and elsewhere, it's now a global phenome-
non. The desert caravan is a different thing today.

Toad, in Kenneth Grahame's *The Wind in the Willows*, shows
his friends the Toad Hall stable yard; 'and there, drawn out of
the coach house into the open, they saw a gipsy caravan, shining
with newness, painted a canary-yellow picked out with green,
and red wheels. "There you are!" cried Toad, straddling and
expanding himself. "There's real life for you, embodied in that
little cart. The open road, the dusty highway, the heath, the
common, the hedgerows, the rolling downs!"' Something of the
magic persists in Deborah Moggach's *Driving in the Dark* (1989),
where an unhappy bloke drives his empty tourist 'coach', a
Panorama Elite, around England in search of a son he's never
seen. But this is a bus, not a caravan; and Mary Shepherd's
refuge in Alan Bennett's *The Lady in the Van* (1989) is a
Dormobile-type camper, not a proper caravan either — though
at one point she starts 'hankering after a caravan trailer and has
just missed one she saw in *Exchange and Mart*: "They said it
was sold, only they may have thought I was just an old
tramp."' Lewycka, however, features the real thing in one of its
guises, the mobile home for seasonal workers: 'The first thing
I noticed was the light — the dazzling salty light dancing on
the sunny field, the ripening strawberries, the little rounded
caravan perched up on the hill and the oblong boxy caravan
down in the corner, the woods beyond.' The one on the hill, the
women's caravan, is a Swift 'like a fat white hen'; the boxy one,
the men's caravan, is 'a static Everglade in pale green, the sort
you can hire ready-sited in scores of windswept caravan parks
on cliff tops . . . propped up on bricks since one of the wheels
had gone missing.' And of course there are caravan diners,
cafés and studio spaces, temporary accommodation for rock
festivals, circuses and film crews, transient permanencies beyond
tourism and nomadism — all hinting, topically, at alternative,
affordable housing of plywood and aluminium. Design and
décor, if any, are a study in themselves; and the intimate, fragile,
mildly adventurous character of all such sanctuaries seems to
induce daydreams and extraneous thought. Those abandoned

clifftop ones seem intended for this purpose; and after dark you could lie listening to the sea — which, says Proust in *Les Plaisirs et les jours* (*Pleasures and Regrets*, tr. Louise Varese), 'has the charm of things which do not fall silent at night; which, in the midst of our unquiet lives, give us the right to sleep, the assurance that everything will not be annihilated'.

The man who runs the funfair on the Pier Road — dodgems, swings, hobbyhorses, a merry-go-round — lives in a much-travelled wooden four-wheeled caravan built by his father, who ran the show before him. Decorated outside with an awning, flower baskets and copper water cans, it's an exotic presence right in the centre of town, and entirely traditional of its kind. But what of the future? We can recondition caravans and re-cycle them, whole or in part, as stables and garden sheds; or, suggests Hammond, adapt them to an energy-conscious era with lighter materials, solar panels, nuclear-powered fridges and hydrogen-burning stoves. Instead of plywood, something made from crops, something biodegradable like Ryvita. You could just eat them, I suppose, when they fall to bits. They've great potential, certainly, in the new age of migration. Lewycka captures this with her international cast of characters imported from Ukraine, Poland, China, Malawi: the whole world is on the move, and the summer roads are choked with caravans. But the derelict ones aren't going anywhere any more. One can only imagine the benighted interiors, like the empty house in Virginia Woolf's *To the Lighthouse*: 'So with the lamps put out, the moon sunk, and a thin rain drumming on the roof, a down-pouring of immense darkness began . . . ' Then, at dawn in *The Waves*: 'The sun fell in sharp wedges inside the room. Whatever the light touched became dowered with a fanatical existence.' A *fanatical* existence!

'Caravan Park Closure' (*Irish Times*, 26/8/16): 'Up to 100 low-income residents of a caravan park in Greystones, Co. Wicklow, face homelessness, having been given notice to quit by their landlord Haven Homes, due to financial circumstances.' Deteriorating conditions and legislative changes have made them uneconomic. 'Down a narrow lane off the Bray-Greystones cliff walk', these structures are no longer sustainable. A local activist says the County Council should purchase the land and renovate the homes; but will this happen? You could probably build a new hotel up there, and a culture of property development aims only at profit. Once a viable alternative, even caravans are decreasingly so; alternatives are closing down everywhere. The more reason to cherish abandoned caravans, wherever they are, and not just for their picturesque qualities (though many artists and photographers find them irresistible) but for their 'spiritual' dimensions too. They remain symbolic, if no longer practical, in the high-rise building-site and car-park world we inhabit now: somewhere to go in the mind and listen to woods and sea — the sea which, says Proust, 'rejoices the soul because, like the soul, it is an infinite and ineffable aspiration': the tidal aspiration (note the etymology), musical or bronchitic with shingle, the desire of the wave for the moon, which is the rhythm of life itself.

Horizons

A white van dashes past. 'Cleaning Solutions', it reads, 'in pursuit of global excellence.' Biscuits are made with 'joy'. Excellence and joy are now trade terms; 'horizon' too. What with training schemes and management speak, horizons, always figuratively useful — new horizons, broader horizons, time horizons — have a busier metaphorical life than ever. They're especially good for adding a touch of mystery to the banal (what lies beyond the horizon?) but are often themselves banal, and in art can verge on kitsch: it's a risky proposition. Beyond the horizon lie other horizons, each as ephemeral as the last; but the ephemeral is fascinating in itself. Waves slide and dance continuously out there, while what we see from the shore is only a straight line, often choppy, dividing sea from sky. A rough stretch of water presents itself as plane geometry; and a strange residue of flat-earth thinking, somewhere in the genes, sees horizons as a form of enclosure. We note surface activity — surfers, white sails, container ships — and imagine water temperatures and the Gulf Stream which, driven by prevailing winds, can move at a hundred miles a day and still be warm when it reaches us. Boundary, margin, limit, edge, says Roget; perimeter, skyline, rim. Horizons are all these things and more. They're where we live; they're there wherever we go, be they land, sea or city roof horizons. Symbolic land horizons include sand desert, that enigmatic, ocean-like phenomenon. Paul Bowles, in his strange, slow-moving Algerian novel *The Sheltering Sky* (1949), gets close to it: (Kit) 'touched the window-pane; it was ice-cold. The bus bumped and swayed as it continued upward across the plateau . . . Here in the desert, even more than at sea, she had the impression that she was on the top of a great table, that the horizon was the brink of space.' She experiences the

Sahara as an existential extremity.

Considered philosophically, horizons present us with a paradox, confining and liberating our vision at the same time; nor are they real, or only momentarily so. While gratifying visual expectation, they remain imaginative constructs, fictions; the closer to them we get the more they recede, the more *far-fetched* they seem. Between the bright edge, that slight meniscus, and the immediate foreground, what dark depths, what intensity! Surrounded by land horizons (a line of hills, fields, houses, woods), why do we think primarily of *sea* horizons? Because they're open, and because popular culture of the early 20th century, heyday of ocean travel, looked on them with such favour. Gaelic poets scanned them once for aid from overseas, but they seem not to have interested Shakespeare, for example, a Warwickshire man, who gives them no specific mention where you'd most expect, in *The Tempest* and so on; or Defoe (Crusoe is too busy to gaze out to sea), or the 18th century, except for those Gaelic poets and William Cowper, when the modern sailing and swimming cults had yet to establish themselves, as they soon did with Byron and the rest. The rise of 19th-century imperialism gave horizons a new significance: all that tonnage racing back and forth to India and China. Their popularity peaked in the 1930s, those hard times, with the likes of Ernst Lubitsch's flighty movie *Monte Carlo* (1930), where Jeanette MacDonald sings 'Beyond the Blue Horizon' (lyrics by Leo Robin), and James Hilton's best-selling novel *Lost Horizon* (1933), which exploited the romance of long-distance flight and introduced the world to 'Shangri-La'. Proust was on to horizons early. A boy, though a precocious one, Marcel watches the evening sea from his hotel room at Balbec (*À l'ombre des jeunes filles en fleurs*, the Scott Moncrieff translation): 'Sometimes the ocean filled almost the whole of my window, raised as it was by a band of sky edged at the top only by a line the same blue as the sea, so that I supposed it to be still sea, and the change in colour due only to some effect of lighting. Another day the sea was painted only in the lower part of the window, all the rest of which was filled with so many clouds, packed one against another in horizontal bands, that its panes seemed . . . to be presenting a "Cloud Study".'

They cry out, as in Proust, for artistic representation; and more than this, for they work too as a *compositional* principle in art, what with frames and framing devices or their absence. (Howard Hodgkin painted on the frames themselves, and now we have the 'expanded field' of art outside the box.) The realistic horizon as compositional principle has been a feature of landscape painting at least since the 17th century of Claude and Ruisdael. Sarah Iremonger, a contemporary artist, once put it like this: 'The vertical line suggests an actual presence, a being, whereas the horizontal line describes a place for that being to exist.' She worked in the vertical for several years: dark upright panels — blues, greens — aspiring to black as in 'Blue Light' (1994) and 'Night Light' (1995). She has also worked in the horizontal: often a deep dark sea and a cloudy sky, laterally trisected, a hint of light at the horizon itself, but not really representational, 'not pictures of horizons but experiments with paint'. In there too is a 'literary' component. A close reader of Burke's *Philosophical Enquiry* (1767) and related things, she warms to the nature of the 'sublime' as embodied in vastness and infinity; in horizons. Real horizons? No, schematic horizons: we're not talking about seascapes here but about artscapes, even thoughtscapes. 'This new idea,' said Mondrian of abstraction, 'will ignore the particulars of appearance, that is to say, natural form and colour; on the contrary, it should find its expression in the *abstraction* of form and colour.' Iremonger now appropriates and disrupts this aesthetic, and the framing functions of colour and form. Her horizons define themselves not in realistic, or even abstract terms, but in imaginative ones: what lies beyond. What lies beyond perceived reality, the received frame of reference? *Shifting* frames, ontological alternatives, deep-water mysteries, drowned forests, shipwrecks, *Star Wars*, vanished continents?

Marie Heaney, in *Over Nine Waves* (1994), renders a famous moment in the story of Niamh and Oisín (Finn Cycle) as follows: 'Ahead of them they saw a most delightful country bathed in sunshine, spread out in all its splendour. Set amid the smooth rich plains was a majestic fortress that shone like a prism in the sun. Surrounding it were airy halls and summer-houses built with great artistry and inlaid with precious stones.' The pair have arrived at Tír na nÓg where nobody grows old and sorrow is unknown. (The name survives in that of a beach-front resort in Antigua, a folk band, and video games including the techno-fascist *Mystic Knights of Tír na nÓg*.) But this shining destination is only one of several imaginary places in the Atlantic. Hy-Brasil, supposedly a circular island a hundred miles or so off the southwest of Ireland, appeared on maps as late as the 19th century. Dodging sea monsters and waterspouts, St. Brendan went in search of it, says the *Navigatio*. Perhaps there *was* once such an island, since submerged by rising sea levels or subsidence of the sea bed. Paul Simons, in *Weird Weather* (1996), describes thermal inversions, mirages caused by weather: 'When conditions are calm and warm air sits on top of cool air it creates a "temperature inversion" which behaves like a mirror, bending light and . . . revealing places hidden by the curve of the earth.' The early Christian writers endowed such apparitions with religious significance ('Brendan' speaks):

> *I passed the voiceless anchorites, their isles,*
> *Saw the ice-palaces upon the seas,*
> *Mentioned Christ's name to men cut off from men,*
> *Heard the whales snort, and saw the Kraken!*
> — Padraic Colum, 'The Burial of Saint Brendan'

Uí Breasil, O'Brasil, the Breasal country, was named for St. Bresal (6th c.), a friend of Brendan, or perhaps for St. Bresal (8th c.), once an abbot of Iona. Isola or Insula de Brazil appears on 14th-c. maps and stayed there at the same spot for centuries. Shortly after its disappearance from 'history', if not from myth and legend, Brunel's *Great Eastern* laid the first successful transatlantic cable from Kerry to Newfoundland. There are many fibre-optic cables now, and no doubt that's good news. Rachel Carson reported the bad news decades ago in a famous preface to the 1960 reissue of *The Sea Around Us* (1951), where she warned about the future of radioactive material: 'By its very vastness and its seeming remoteness, the sea has invited the attention of those who have the problem of disposal, and with very little discussion and almost no public notice . . . has been selected as a "natural" burying place for contaminated rubbish.' It doesn't seem so as you look out at the waves and contemplate the horizon; but these things — drowned forests, shipwrecks, mythical lands, cables and nuclear waste — lie there in the subconscious, of which the Big Blue is a famously potent symbol.

We hear a different music of the spheres according to where we sit in the auditorium, said Einstein; and we see a different horizon according to where we stand on the shore. This relativity, and related deflections, inform Iremonger's post-conceptual art. Working, for example, from digitally manipulated versions of traditional paintings, or from photographs of the sea as seen from Cobh, looking south over the Cork Harbour area, she uses deconstructive 'colour separations' to create images which are themselves horizons of thought. Nothing definitely *is*, everything is becoming; vision becomes re-vision, brine becomes watercolour: 'I am painting about the horizons of painting, not horizons themselves as a subject but painting as the subject.' So instead of familiar horizons, though she starts from these, we get *event* horizons of a kind, where previous convictions vanish, to be replaced by fragmentation (screensaver tiles) and *re*-construction, psychic flow, indeterminacy, unknowable futures. I could have wished for a few gulls; but these artworks — paintings, photos, neon drawings — chart a voyage from the interior to the open sea and, while remaining themselves, document new dimensions and expanding fields of creative possibility, wherever the edge may be.

Olympia and the Internet

There were three girls and three boys in my mother's family. The whole bunch retired to Bangor in old age, but my early memories of them relate to 'Hilltop', above Glengormley, when the grandparents were still alive. Willie, my 'wicked' uncle, was the eldest, and died relatively young. Roy, the youngest, lived to be ninety. He and Willie, like others in the extended family, were at sea during 'the War', and I must have been four or five before I was properly conscious of this Roy in a Merchant Navy uniform cap I coveted. He was an unimposing figure with a plain, frank, friendly face; but he had brains. Having left school for apprenticeship at sixteen, he had little formal education except of a technical nature, but later turned himself into that once familiar type, the self-taught 'eccentric'. He worked for an Edinburgh-based marine insurance firm and, when not on his travels, sat scribbling in his study. His chief interests were science and maths, but he found time for literature: Tolstoy, Gorky, Sinclair Lewis. (Unusually too, for an Ulster Protestant household, he'd an Irish-English dictionary in his shelves.) He subscribed to film magazines, belonged to a film society, and at one stage kept up with European cinema. He was thought to fancy a neighbouring Margerie Laird, but no: with three sisters to spoil him he stayed a bachelor and lived at home. He knew something of finance and invested their pensions for them, with striking results. He was, of course, resolutely left-wing, and he had a typewriter: an old Imperial, standard size, on which he typed up his insurance reports. I'd often bike up there for left-wingery — to which, perhaps naively, I adhere — and for typing practice, the clunk and clink, the sumptuous black register (even now, though, I only use four fingers and a thumb). Type-writers in my life: an acoustic Adler; an electric Remington, a present; and now again a manual, also a present. The Remington was great while it lasted. Paul Auster avoided electricals, he says, 'the constant hum of the motor, the jitterbug pulse of alternating current vibrating in my fingers'. I *liked* the brisk vitality of the Remington, but my working life is calmer now. Staring out over the keyboard, I take longer choosing a word, and pause at punctuation (comma or semi-colon?); the machine is patient, and instils patience. It chatters when it's excited but promotes more generous time values, and its usual mode is a tactful silence. Unlike the contemporary playstation it doesn't beep and it doesn't hector. A 20th-century device, a relic of the industrial era, fit only for derision and dereliction, it's not to be taken seriously in the age of Google and tweet, yet it still *works*. Works better, maybe, after so much experience, despite the dust and fluff it secretes in the undercarriage; and it's not designed to distract. An antique but, like so many antiques, it has personality, even character — which it needs in order to live in a hyper-connected time. She's an elegant old girl who hasn't lost the regal air of her youth, who remains trim and goes by the name Olympia.

Roy would have loved the internet. A sucker for any kind of mechanical contrivance, he'd have taken to high tech like a duck to water; but he was too old to *think different* when the world went digital. Even I, twenty years his junior, was too old; or perhaps too lazy. An analogue simpleton, I couldn't be bothered with all that complicated stuff. (Technology sees me coming and starts acting up.) Besides, I was suspicious and never trusted the internet for an instant. Something to do with its strategical origins as military hardware, software; the gold rush, the hysteria, the data-mining, the intrusive sense of entitlement. It wants to know everything about everyone everywhere — for commercial reasons and perhaps for more sinister, political ones. This global bubble has been compared to Borges' Library of Babel, whose polished surfaces 'represent and promise the infinite'; and Amazon gave publishers worldwide just two weeks (in August) to opt *out* of its own vast online library. It ain't ethical; it sure takes us farther down the road to the promised infinity, but infinity is not of this earth. What we're talking about here is 'reality distortion' (Google-speak) as a marketable commodity. Nothing new in that of course, except that the commodifiable now includes our own thoughts and daily lives, which we yield up in tribute to the networks with our websites, emails and online conversations. Not only our smartphones but our minds are tapped, with 'no concept of deletion'. Nothing new in that either. William Gibson, who coined the term cyberspace — 'a consensual hallucination' — foresaw all this as long ago as his first novel *Neuromancer* (1984), with its techno-spooks and video games, nerve-splicing and bionics. Bionics, though, are as old as body armour, and certainly as old as Myles na gCopaleen: 'Remington I knew well. He had the whole of his insides taken out of him, bones and all . . . and had new bones made for him out of old typewriters', followed by a complete typewriter replacement in middle age. Sometimes, says Myles, 'he would accidentally tap down a key or two when leaning against counters or bridge parapets'. Myles can be weirdly prescient when he gets up a head of steam.

Apple ('Think Different') pretends, or used to pretend, to countercultural *chic*; but, as one former employee put it, 'What exactly are Apple countering? They *are* the culture now.' And a profoundly hypocritical culture it is too. The objectionable Steve Jobs, 'the original tech hipster, who idolized Bob Dylan and spent a summer in an ashram', says Andrew Keen in *The Internet Is Not the Answer* (2015), also outsourced the manufacture of Apple products to a notoriously inhumane Chinese megafactory; and Apple, like Google, has been playing tax-avoidance games on a vast scale since its inception. So how do we *think differently*? We fight these giants with regulation, and with the determination they themselves deploy in the furtherance of their aims. Either that or disconnect, secede. Secede, or never get involved in the first place. Were Roy alive today he'd be in an electronic file somewhere. My own solution: the steam typewriter, though I admit I have friends who can look things up for me online when there's something I don't know (rare, but it happens). Even the innocent t/w is technology, granted (Gibson bashed out ice-breaking *Neuromancer* on an old portable); even the pen — which, said Marie de Sévigné, 'has always a great part in what we write' — and even the pencil. Slow and tactile, these make for greater consideration and intimacy, a more personal medium. It may come back to that in time, the Bic and the speckled Conway Stewart; meanwhile my 13mm black nylon ribbons, made in China and distributed from Germany, I get from London (Ryman's) to cover me with ink as I figure out, yet again, the proper way to install them. They have their frustrations, or perhaps I mean the writing does. Typewriters have been violently abused by temperamental authors; but Olympia knows no such theatricals.

'Ineluctable modality of the visible . . . Signatures of all things I am here to read' (Joyce). But high tech introduces, if we let it, a cognitive dissonance between subject and object. Rewired for electronic information, blinded by science, we're in danger of losing touch with primary experience; the unmediated sea-wrack on the strand is even stranger to us than it was to Joyce. Whatever the dire economic and social consequences of the 'digital revolution', and they are many, it's the commodification of thought that's most alarming, that and the robotic invigilation; but there's nothing 'ineluctable' about it. Olympia and I commune with each other in private. I post and receive unopened mail — letters, you know: it can still be done — and nobody taps my phone as far as I know (why would they?). A friend in New York took one or two Arabic lessons before a trip to Dubai, so maybe they tap his: who knows? 'Just because you're paranoid,' as Delmore Schwartz said, 'doesn't mean they're not out to get you.' Sure they are, they want *everyone* in the system; and in America I've been reproached, impatiently even, for not being online, as if this was a serious solecism. To engage with the topic at all is to play an insidious game. It's not neuroscience, much though it claims to be (the ghost eludes the machine), nor is it the new way of thinking and being that the system likes to pretend. The brief space age is over, at least for now; and the internet too will implode in time if not properly regulated: an old model of production masquerading as new. Its infinite magic is mostly commercial hype, a recreational mysticism for ever breaking down. It has its uses of course, and might even help reactivate the radical politics we left behind with the typewriters. Olympia agrees. She doesn't do hegemony or coercion, preferring her own slow pace and modest achievements; and she can boast a distinguished cultural provenance. Most 20th-century literature, after all, was written on typewriters, and they've had an artistic history too: Hopper's 'Office at Night' (1940), Warhol, Hockney. Also a filmic one. Joseph Cotten, in *Citizen Kane* (1941), wakes from a drunken stupor with his head in close-up on a clicking t/w; Diane Keaton, in *Reds* (1981), throws hers out the window; and Ciaran Carson, in *The Star Factory* (1997), re-runs in his head a scene from an old science-fiction dystopia where 'phalanxes of nearly identical typists are overlooked by huge art-deco clocks with blips for numerals, and are overseen by white-coated centurions with clipboards. The typing pool is the size of an aircraft hangar or a movie studio, and all the girl extras who are acting the typists want to be Hollywood stars.'

Just as the pen, according to Mme de Sévigné, has always a part in what we write, so too had (has) the typewriter. Henry James's periphrastic late style, for example, has been ascribed to dictation. The typist had her work cut out:

> *Not yet so much as this morning had she felt herself sink into possession, gratefully glad that the warmth of the southern summer was still in the high florid rooms, palatial chambers where hard cool pavements took reflexions in their lifelong polish, and where the sun on the stirred sea-water, flickering up through open windows, played over the painted "subjects" in the splendid ceilings . . . all toned with time and all flourished and scolloped and gilded about, set in their moulded and figured concavity (a nest of white cherubs, friendly creatures of the air) and appreciated by the aid of that second tier of lights, straight openings to the front, which did everything, even with the Baedekers and photographs, to make the place an apartment of state.*
>
> (The Wings of the Dove, 1902)

William Burrough's aleatoric methods must have been suggested, at some level, by his family background: a grandfather who founded the Burroughs Adding Machine Co. (St. Louis), later the Burroughs Corporation. Truman Capote, asked about Kerouac's *On the Road*, snapped, 'That's not writing, that's typing.' Concrete poems, t/w-inspired, have been around for ages; and now we have computer verse written on, to and about computers, besides the old manual stuff. Poetry, that strange persistent art made up — ideally — of soul, song and formal necessity, survives and even thrives in the digital age; thrives, perhaps, *because* of digitization. It's a form of resistance, or should be, an insistence on private truth and fantasy in the face of a dominant paradigm that, increasingly invading public space, drives us indoors to paper and pen. And Olympia? After the chatter she is calm, her keys at rest, perhaps a little tired from all the things she's written, perhaps bored by the hard copy she's been turning out today and which she's been the first to read.